INTERMEDIATE LISTENING COMPREHENSION

Understanding and Recalling Spoken English

Third Edition

Patricia Dunkel   **Phyllis L. Lim**

HEINLE
CENGAGE Learning

Australia • Brazil • Japan • Korea • Mexico • Singapore • Spain • United Kingdom • United States

HEINLE
CENGAGE Learning™

Intermediate Listening Comprehension: Understanding and Recalling Spoken English, Third Edition
Patricia Dunkel, Phyllis L. Lim

Publisher, Adult and Academic ESL:
  James W. Brown

Senior Acquisitions Editor: Sherrise Roehr

Director of Product Development:
  Anita Raducanu

Director of Marketing: Amy Mabley

Technology Manager: Andrew Christensen

Marketing Manager: Laura Needham

Development Editor: Kasia Zagorski

Editorial Assistant: Katherine Reilly

Production Editor: Chrystie Hopkins

Manufacturing Manager: Marcia Locke

Production Services: Pre-Press Company, Inc.

Cover Designer: Ha Nguyen

Text Designer: Carol Rose

Cover Image: © "Rhythme couleur," 1939 by
  Sonia Delaunay, © L & M SERVICES
  B.V. Amsterdam 20040502

Photo: R.G. Ojeda, Musee des Beaux-Arts, Lille,
  France, © Reunion des Musees Nationaux/
  Art Resources, NY.

Library of Congress Control Number: 2004117882

ISBN-13: 978-1-4130-0397-0

ISBN-10: 1-4130-0397-4

Heinle
20 Channel Center Street
Boston, MA 02210
USA

Cengage Learning is a leading provider of customized learning solutions with office locations around the globe, including Singapore, the United Kingdom, Australia, Mexico, Brazil, and Japan. Locate your local office at **www.cengage.com/global**

Cengage Learning products are represented in Canada by Nelson Education, Ltd.

Visit Heinle online at **elt.heinle.com**

Visit our corporate website at **www.cengage.com**

Printed in the United States of America
8 9 10 11 12 15 14 13 12

Contents

We dedicate this book to the enhancement of intercultural communication and international understanding. We thank all the many students that have contributed to our professional and personal development over the years.

Also, a sense of special appreciation and gratitude is extended to our colleagues Kasia McNabb, the guiding spirit of this third edition, Andrew Christensen, our technology guru, and to Jim Brown, our admired editor and long-time friend.

To the Teacher

Overview

Intermediate Listening Comprehension, Third Edition is an intensive training program in listening fluency and comprehension development. In recent years, helping ESL and EFL learners develop their listening comprehension has become a major focus of teaching for several reasons. First, listening plays a key role in the development of a learner's first language (L1), and listening is believed, by extension, to play a prime role in the development of a learner's second language (L2). Rost (2002, p. 81), for example, notes that "we all manage to acquire our first language, and we do it primarily through listening. There is a seamless connection between learning to listen and acquiring our first language (L1)." We acquire listening ability in our first language in a graduated and seemingly effortless way, and regardless of what that first language is, we all tend to acquire it in the about same amount of time, as Rost (2002) notes. We do it through practice and by gaining confidence that we can learn to listen and use the language effectively.

L1 learners usually acquire their L1 with the aid of caretakers/teachers who help them to understand their first language and to reach out to communicate with their caretakers/teachers and other people who speak the language. The caretakers/teachers, in other words, provide the child with "comprehensible input" that gives the child good reason to listen and good reason to make an appropriate response after the message is comprehended. Rost (2002, p. 86) suggests that, among other things, the comprehensible input of the caretakers/teachers helps the L1 (or L2) learners by

- providing a correct model for imitation;
- reducing the processing load by facilitating segmentation of the input into smaller chunks of language, and by simplifying the length, structure, and lexical load modeled in the input;
- clearly enunciating;
- slowing down the speech when necessary, and speeding up when possible;
- directing the learner's attention to the relevant information in the input;
- improving the intelligibility of the language heard;
- providing feedback on the accuracy or inaccuracy of the comprehension;

- promoting a positive affect in the learner toward interaction with others; and finally,

- teaching social routines—or in the case of *Intermediate Listening Comprehension, Third Edition*—rhetorical routines and the signal cues employed by speakers who use one or more of the major rhetorical routines involving Process, Cause and Effect, Definition, and so on.

The scope and sequence of *Intermediate Listening Comprehension, Third Edition* seek to promote development of each of the above listening-facilitation goals with prelistening activities, comprehensible input and while-listening activities, and varied postlistening experiences for the L2 learner. With the aid of a creative teacher, the program can also be used to promote conversational participation about the topics heard and/or the activities done; conversational participation is yet another of the vital skills an L2 (as well as an L1) learner needs to hone in today's world.

In addition to being important for learning a first and second language, developing listening fluency in English is a survival skill in today's globalized world. According to Brownell (2002), technology has increased the number of messages sent and the speed with which they are delivered. In business meetings where English is the language of communication, or in lecture halls where English is the language of instruction, listeners of English must confront a constantly changing and increasingly complex listening environment. In both such surroundings, the ESL/EFL listeners must (1) be able to scan the information they receive in English, (2) be able to determine where to focus their attention in the stream of speech, and, (3) be able to make sense of what they hear. Often, they must make a written or spoken response to demonstrate that they have processed the message correctly. As Brownell (2002) notes, something can go wrong at *any* stage during this listening process. If something does go wrong, and comprehension fails, it can be expensive for the ESL/EFL learner in terms of money, time, grades, and even personal relationships. On the other hand, if people become stronger and more accurate comprehenders of English, they stand to profit personally, in business meetings or in the lecture halls of college campuses.

For students of English for Academic Purposes (EAP), the need to develop listening fluency in English is critical. EAP learners need to practice listening to various types of extended discourse so they can develop the ability to understand, remember, and evaluate the information heard in their lectures. EAP learners will also be called on to demonstrate that they understand the messages in the lectures and that they are able to understand, remember, interpret, and select whatever is relevant in the stream of the EAP discourse. To do all this, they need to practice listening in English, and, at the same time, they need to *enjoy* the experience of enhancing and expanding their listening skills!

The authors of *Intermediate Listening Comprehension, Third Edition* hope that they have provided a listening program that will help L2 listeners make their listening comprehension of English stronger.

We very much hope that the L2 listeners will gain the confidence needed to listen to streams of English at both slower and speedier paces. More specifically, the authors of *Intermediate Listening Comprehension, Third Edition* seek to familiarize the listener with the major rhetorical patterns of formal, spoken English. College-bound students especially need to become familiar with these patterns and with the signal cues and text structures the speaker uses in lecture (or minilecture) speech. As a result, each unit of *Intermediate Listening Comprehension, Third Edition* models one or more of these patterns and gives examples of the vocabulary and signal cues associated with the various rhetorical patterns contained in the minilectures and activities.

In summary, *Intermediate Listening Comprehension, Third Edition* seeks to improve L2 learners' listening comprehension by 1) providing samples of clearly enunciated, slower-paced speech, as well as more extemporaneous and authentic-sounding speech; 2) helping learners recognize the cue signals for the five targeted rhetorical patterns; and 3) providing a variety of task-oriented and enjoyable listening and speaking activities.

New to This Edition

A new feature added to the third edition of *Intermediate Listening Comprehension* is a video component. The initial listening for each chapter is now available on DVD or VHS. The video is meant to be used as a complement to the traditional audio program. Students may opt to view lecturers delivering the chapter lectures in order to simulate a more authentic classroom listening experience.

Also new to the third edition are additional **Listening Factoids** Each chapter now contains two high-interest listening bits on topics related to the chapter theme.

Organization of the Program

Intermediate Listening Comprehension, Third Edition has five units which focus on the following rhetorical patterns:

   I. Chronology
  II. Process
 III. Definition/Classification
  IV. Comparison/Contrast
   V. Casual Analysis

Each unit is graded in terms of length and difficulty of grammatical structures used in the talk. Each of the units consists of three chapters. Each chapter is organized into three sections:

Prelistening

  A. Listening Preparation
  B. Preview of Vocabulary and Sentences
  C. Rhetorical Listening Cues

Listening

    A. Initial Listening

    B. Mental Rehearsal and Review of the Talk

    C. Consolidation

Postlistening

    A. The Comprehension Check

        1. Recognizing Information and Checking Accuracy

        2. Using and Expanding on the Information in the Talk

            a. Recapping the Information from Your Notes

            b. Expanding on the Information in the Talk

    B. The Listening Expansion

        (a variety of listening tasks)

    C. The Listening Factoids

The Instructional Design of Each Chapter

Prelistening

A. Listening Preparation. This initial portion activates the student's world knowledge to help him or her predict the content and course of the discourse. The student is prepared for the talk he or she will hear and is asked to focus on the topic of the discourse. Evocation of mental imagery is attempted in this preparatory stage.

B. Preview of Vocabulary and Sentences. Here, students focus on the low frequency and/or story-specific vocabulary with a gloss and then the item in the talk-specific context.

C. Rhetorical Listening Cues. Finally, this section highlights the specific vocabulary, structures and organization of the particular rhetorical pattern used during the talk.

Listening

A. Initial Listening. This section presents the listening passage in its entirety. A natural pace and clear delivery is used by the speaker.

B. Mental Rehearsal and Review of the Talk. Now, the student is provided with the opportunity to review and mentally rehearse the essential message units of the talk. The rehearsal allows for chunking of the information contained in the talk. The student repeats the units subvocally, concentrating on the comprehension and recall of information presented in the talk.

C. Consolidation.* This final segment presents the message units reinserted into the contextual and syntactic whole of the talk. The

---

* The script of the Consolidation will vary somewhat from the script of the Initial Listening because of paraphrasing and inclusion of restarts, verbal fillers, and restatements reflective of more authentic spoken discourse.

speaker uses redundancies, reiteration, and verbal fillers in the presentation. Students can take notes during the paced presentation if they wish.

Postlistening

A. The Comprehension Check

1. Recognizing Information and Checking Accuracy. Here, students check their comprehension and recall of the factual information contained in the talk. The student becomes familiar with standard oral-comprehension testing formats, including multiple-choice items, true-false statements, short answer questions, etc.

2. Using and Expanding on the Information in the Talk
   a. Recapping the Information from Your Notes. This activity offers students the opportunity to recount the information in the talk with the aid of their notes.
   b. Expanding on the Information in the Talk. This portion allows students to interact with other students, expressing their own ideas and opinions on a variety of topics related to the lecture.

B. The Listening Expansion

Tasks 1 and 2 can be completed only by carefully listening to the directions and information given orally. The listening task exercises spiral through previously presented rhetorical patterns, vocabulary, and structures, and also present novel listening and testing experiences.

C. The Listening Factoids

The two Listening Factoids present novel, high-interest, sometimes surprising facts related to the topic of the chapter. Students listen to absorb interesting bits of information or trivia to ponder or discuss, as appropriate.

Photos and Illustrations

Each unit has a general thematic photo that visually develops the theme of the talk.

Illustrations also accompany numerous Listening Expansion exercises.

References

Brownell, J. (2002). *Listening: Attitudes, Principles, and Skills* (2nd ed.). Boston: Allyn and Bacon.

Rost, M. (2002). *Teaching and Researching Listening*. New York: Longman.

INTERMEDIATE LISTENING COMPREHENSION

Focus on:

Chronology

Chronology is a way of telling something in the order in which it happened. Chronology is used to tell stories and to relate historical events.

Napoleon:
From Schoolboy to Emperor

I. PRELISTENING

A. Listening Preparation

You are going to listen to a story about Napoleon Bonaparte, the French conqueror. Think about the man for a minute. Do you have a picture of him in your mind? What did he look like? Was he a tall man? No, he was really quite short, but he was a very powerful man. Some people think he was a great man—a hero. Other people think he was a villain—a very bad person. But most people agree that he was one of the most important men in European history.

B. Preview of Vocabulary and Sentences

emperor the ruler of an empire
- Napoleon was a French soldier who became *emperor* of the French Empire.

military school a school that trains young people to be soldiers or officers
- Napoleon's father sent him to *military school* in France.

to excel to do better than others
- Napoleon *excelled* in mathematics and in military science.

career an occupation followed as one's lifework

fame recognition; distinction; great honor
- Napoleon began the military *career* that brought him *fame*, power, riches, and finally defeat.

victories conquests; successes
- Napoleon won many, many military *victories*.

to control to have power over; to govern by domination
- At one time Napoleon *controlled* most of Europe.

to lose to fail to keep; to be unable to save
- In the military campaign into Russia, Napoleon *lost* most of his army.

to be deserted to be left by people who do not plan to return; to be abandoned
- The great French conqueror died alone—*deserted* by his family and his friends.

C. Rhetorical Listening Cues

In this talk the speaker tells you about the life of Napoleon. The story is told in chronological order; that is, the events are related in the order in which they happened. The story begins with Napoleon's birth in 1769 and ends with his death in 1821. Listen for what happened when Napoleon was 10 years old, 16 years old, and 24 years old. Another time expression you will hear that shows chronology is "several years later."

II. LISTENING

🎧 A. Initial Listening

Now let's listen to a talk about the Emperor Napoleon. It may help you to concentrate on the talk if you close your eyes while you listen. Just relax and listen carefully.

🎧 B. Mental Rehearsal and Review of the Talk

All right. Let's listen to the talk once again. This time, the talk will be given in message units. Please repeat each unit to yourself silently after you hear it. Remember, don't say the units out loud.

🎧 C. Consolidation

You will hear the talk given once again. This time as you listen, take notes on what you hear.

III. POSTLISTENING

🎧 A. The Comprehension Check

1. Recognizing Information and Checking Accuracy

For questions 1–4 you will hear multiple-choice questions about the information presented in the talk. Listen to each question and decide whether (a), (b), (c), or (d) is the best answer to the question.

_____ 1. (a) in 1769
      (b) in 1821
      (c) in France
      (d) on Corsica

_____ 2. (a) outstanding
      (b) excellent
      (c) good
      (d) poor

_____ 3. (a) power
      (b) wealth
      (c) defeat
      (d) all of the above

_____ 4. (a) when he was 51 years old
      (b) just before he defeated England
      (c) after his military campaign into Russia
      (d) several years after he became a general

For questions 5–8 you will hear statements about the life of Napoleon. If the statement is true, put a T on the line next to the number of the statement. If the statement you hear is false, put an F on the line, and explain why the statement is false.

CHECK YOUR ANSWERS ▶   5. _____   6. _____   7. _____   8. _____

2. Using and Expanding on the Information in the Talk

a. Recapping the Information from Your Notes. Use your notes to recap the information you learned about the life of Napoleon. Present the information to the class or to one of your classmates.

b. Expanding on the Information in the Talk. Discuss with a classmate why you agree (or do not agree) with the following statements:

1. Napoleon was a great man.

2. It would be impossible today for a person like Napoleon to become powerful enough to conquer and rule so many countries.

3. The only way a country can be safe is to have a powerful military to protect itself.

4. Every young man and woman should be required to do at least two years of military service for his or her country.

⌢ B. The Listening Expansion

Task 1.   **Completing a Map**

Look at the map on the following page. It is a picture of the various European kingdoms and empires that existed in Napoleon's time. You are going to fill in the information that is not already on the map. Listen and fill in the missing information.

Task 2.   **Answering Questions about the Completed Map**

Now the map is complete. Here are some questions about the map of Napoleonic Europe. When you hear a question, look at the map to find the answer to the question you hear. Listen for the words "north," "south," "east," or "west." Write the answer to the question on the appropriate blank line.

For example, you will hear the question: "What was the name of the empire that was south of the Austrian Empire in Napoleon's time?" The answer to the question is "the Ottoman Empire." You must complete the rest of the answers. Are you ready? Do you have the map handy for consultation? Good. Let's begin.

1. _____

2. _____

3. _____

4. _____

CHECK YOUR ANSWERS ▶   5. _____

LISTENING FACTOIDS

#1 Napoleon led a very exciting and dangerous life, but he died in his own bed. The cause of Napoleon's death has been the subject of controversy from that time to the present. Listen to some of the theories people have had about the cause of his death.

#2 Powerful men in history leave behind a number of sayings that linger long after they are dead. Listen to seven of Napoleon's famous sayings, or "words of wisdom." Each saying will be repeated twice.

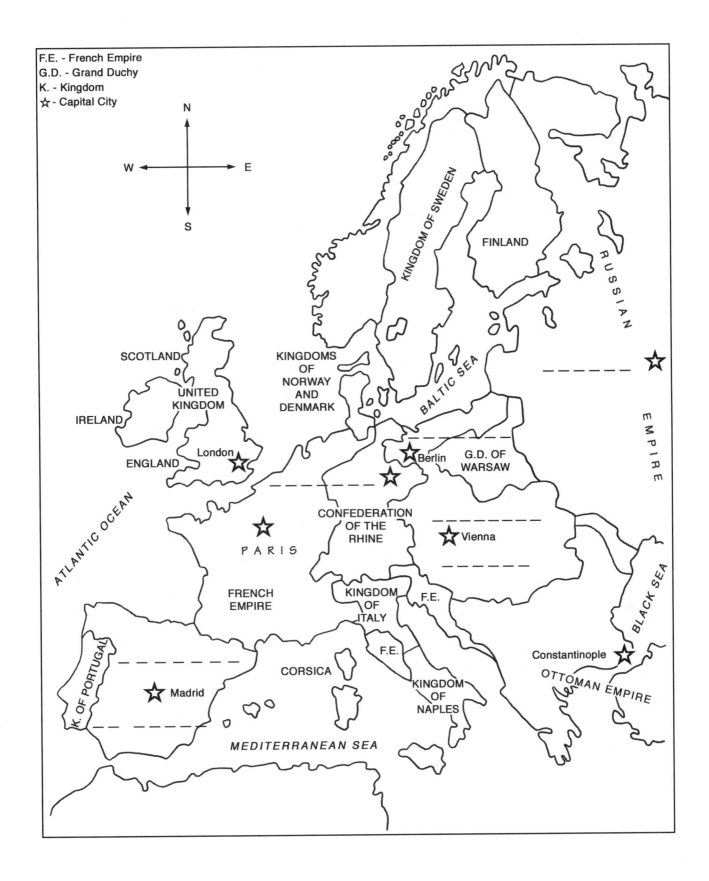

F.E. - French Empire
G.D. - Grand Duchy
K. - Kingdom
☆ - Capital City

N
W E
S

KINGDOM OF SWEDEN

FINLAND

RUSSIAN

SCOTLAND

KINGDOMS
OF
NORWAY
AND
DENMARK

BALTIC SEA

EMPIRE

UNITED
KINGDOM

IRELAND

ENGLAND

London ☆

☆ Berlin

G.D. OF
WARSAW

CONFEDERATION
OF THE
RHINE

☆ Vienna

ATLANTIC OCEAN

☆

PARIS

FRENCH
EMPIRE

KINGDOM
OF
ITALY

F.E.

BLACK SEA

K. OF PORTUGAL

☆ Madrid

CORSICA

F.E.

KINGDOM
OF
NAPLES

Constantinople ☆

OTTOMAN EMPIRE

MEDITERRANEAN SEA

Pompeii:
Destroyed, Forgotten, and Found

I. PRELISTENING

A. Listening Preparation

You are going to listen to a story about the ancient city of Pompeii. What do you know about Pompeii? Do you know where it was located? Do you know why it is famous? What happened in Pompeii? Why did many people die there? Why do tourists visit Pompeii today?

B. Preview of Vocabulary and Sentences

Bay of Naples
- Pompeii was located on the ocean, on the *Bay of Naples*.

79 C.E. 79 years after the birth of Christ
- In the year *79 C.E.,* a young Roman boy was visiting his uncle in Pompeii.

sight a scene; a view
- Pliny saw a frightening *sight*.

ash residue left when material is consumed by fire; very small particles of mineral matter that a volcano sends out
- Rock and *ash* flew through the air.

to flee to run to escape from danger
- Many people were able *to flee* the city and to escape death.

to be buried alive to be covered by ash or dirt completely while still living and then to die
- These unlucky people were *buried alive* under the ash.

to dig to turn up the ground or soil with a shovel
- An Italian farmer was *digging* on his farm.

archaeologists scientists who study the remains of ancient civilizations
- *Archaeologists* began to excavate—to dig—in the area.

ruins the remains of destroyed buildings or cities
- Today tourists come from all over the world to see the *ruins* of the famous city of Pompeii.

C. Rhetorical Listening Cues

In this talk the speaker tells you a story about the ancient city of Pompeii. This story begins about 2,000 years ago and continues up to today. The story is told in chronological order. Listen for dates such as "79 C.E." and time expressions such as "for about three days," "as time went by," and "for 1,700 years." These time expressions and dates will help you to understand the sequence or order of events in the story.

II. LISTENING

🎧 A. Initial Listening

Now let's listen to a talk about the destroyed city of Pompeii. It may help you to concentrate on the talk if you close your eyes while you listen. Just relax and listen carefully.

🎧 B. Mental Rehearsal and Review of the Talk

All right. Let's listen to the talk once again. This time, the talk will be given in message units. Please repeat each unit to yourself *silently* after you hear it. Remember, don't say the units out loud.

🎧 C. Consolidation

You will hear the talk given once again. This time as you listen, take notes on what you hear.

III. POSTLISTENING

🎧 A. The Comprehension Check

1. Recognizing Information and Checking Accuracy

You will hear five questions about the story. Listen to each question and then write the correct answer to each question in the space provided. Write short answers. (There are several possible answers to some questions.)

1. _____

2. _____

3. _____

4. _____

5. _____

For questions 6–11 you will hear statements about the destruction of Pompeii. If the statement is true, put a *T* on the line next to the number of the statement. If the statement is false, put an *F* on the line, and explain why the statement is false.

CHECK YOUR ANSWERS ▶

6. ____   7. ____   8. ____   9. ____   10. ____   11. ____

2. Using and Expanding on the Information in the Talk

a. Recapping the Information from Your Notes.   Use your notes to recap the information you learned about the eruption of the volcano on ancient Pompeii. Present the information to the class or to one of your classmates.

b. Expanding on the Information in the Talk.   Discuss with a classmate the following topics:

1. In your opinion, what is the most dangerous man-made disaster facing the world, and what do you think we can do about it?

2. Describe the worst storm, flood, or natural disaster you (or one of your friends or relatives) ever survived?

3. What should you do to save your life if you find yourself in the following situations?
   (a) You are sitting on a beach on the coast of Indonesia and suddenly realize that a tidal wave is coming.
   (b) You are visiting Pompeii to see the ruins and Mt. Vesuvius suddenly erupts with great force.
   (c) You are visiting Miami, Florida and a hurricane occurs.
   (d) You are visiting Oklahoma and a tornado strikes the neighborhood you're living in.
   (e) You are staying in a high-rise hotel in San Francisco, and you feel the hotel tremble and shake because a strong earthquake has hit the city.

4. If I am destined to be in a natural disaster, I would prefer a/an _____ because _____.

5. Hollywood has made many "disaster" movies, such as *The Towering Inferno, The Poseidon Adventure, and Earthquake.* Why do people enjoy watching disaster movies? What is your favorite disaster movie? Why did you enjoy this movie?

∩ B. The Listening Expansion

Task 1.   **Listening for Sequence Identification**

You will hear two sentences—a pair of sentences. Listen carefully and decide if the sentences are given in the correct time sequence. After you listen to each pair of sentences, write *yes* in the space provided if the sentences are in the correct time sequence. Write *no* if the sentences are not in the correct time sequence. Listen to the following two examples.

Example 1. _____   *Example 2.* _____

Are you ready? The following pairs of sentences are from the story about Pompeii. Think about the time sequence in the story.

1. _____   4. _____

2. _____   5. _____

CHECK YOUR ANSWERS ▶   3. _____

Task 2.   **Listening to Complete and Use a Chart**

You are going to complete the following chart about famous volcanoes. Listen to the short lecture and be ready to fill in the information. Follow the instructions in the lecture. At first, you will just listen and look at the chart. I will tell you when to begin to write the information in the blank spaces on the chart. Are you ready?

Famous Volcanoes of the World			
Name	**Location**	**Date of Eruption**	**Approximate Number of People Who Died**
Vesuvius	Italy	79 C.E.	2,000
Cotopaxi	Ecuador	1877	
Krakatoa	Indonesia		36,000
Mont Pelée	Martinique	1902	
Mount St. Helens	Washington State (U.S.A.)	1980	
Mount Tambora	Indonesia		

Now let's use the chart to list the volcanoes in the order of their eruptions. Find the name of the volcano that erupted first in this group of six volcanoes. Write the name of that volcano next to the number 1. Now write the name of the volcano that erupted next according to the dates on the chart. Continue in this way until you have listed the six volcanoes in the order of their eruptions.

1. _____

2. _____

3. _____

4. _____

5. _____

CHECK YOUR ANSWERS ▶

6. _____

LISTENING FACTOIDS

#1 Can a volcano shoot down a plane? Listen to this strange happening.

#2 In his famous letters, Pliny the Younger writes about the death of his uncle who died during the eruption of Mt. Vesuvius. Listen to what happened to the boy's uncle and mentor.

Lance Armstrong:
Survivor and Winner

I. PRELISTENING

A. Listening Preparation

Lance Armstrong secured his place in sporting history in the year 2004 by winning an unprecedented *sixth* consecutive Tour de France cycling competition. Only four other people have won the Tour five times and only one other cyclist has won it five times consecutively. The Tour de France is not only the most prestigious cycling event in the world but also one of the most challenging and grueling contests in all of sports. As amazing as Lance Armstrong's achievements as a cyclist are, his incredible recovery from a near fatal illness and his amazing sporting comeback after his recovery make his life story read like something out of a movie.

B. Preview of Vocabulary and Sentences

competitively in a competitive manner, that is, with the strong purpose of succeeding or winning
- Lance began running and swimming *competitively* when he was only 10 years old.

triathlon a sports contest consisting of three consecutive events (usually swimming, bicycling, and distance running), with no time between events
- By the time he was 13, he was competing in *triathlons* and won the Iron Kids *Triathlon*.

to encourage to support; to fill with courage and confidence
- Lance's mother, who raised Lance mostly by herself, recognized and *encouraged* his competitive spirit.

to focus on to put total attention and energy on
- From that time on, Lance *focused* completely *on* cycling.

amateur a person who participates in an activity or competes for pleasure, *not* for money or for professional reasons
- By 1991, Lance was the U.S. National *Amateur* Champion.

ups and downs good and bad times
- Although he was generally doing very well, Lance had his *ups and downs*.

to be ranked to be placed in a particular order based on some criterion, such as (in sports) the number of games or races won
- By 1996, Lance *was ranked* seventh among cyclists in the world, and he signed a two-year contract with a French racing team.

to be diagnosed to be determined to have a certain, usually medical, condition

to spread to move beyond original place
- At this time, Lance *was diagnosed* with advanced cancer that had already *spread* to his brain and lungs.

surgery a procedure involving cutting the body to repair or remove diseased tissue or organs

aggressive powerful; strong; attacking

chemotherapy a treatment using strong chemicals or drugs to destroy cancerous cells
- After these two *surgeries*, he was given a less than 50-50 chance of survival as he began an *aggressive* three-month course of *chemotherapy*.

sponsor person or organization that supports and assists another person, team, or organization, often financially
- Fortunately, the U.S. Postal Service Team became his new *sponsor*.

comeback a return to an earlier better condition or position
- Lance's big *comeback* was marked by his victory at the 1999 Tour de France.

to be beaten or **to be matched** to be defeated or to be equaled
- Lance's Tour de France record may never *be beaten* or even *be matched*.

to count to matter; to be important
- The book is called *Every Second Counts*, and for Lance, every second has *counted*.

C. Rhetorical Listening Cues

In this talk the speaker narrates the story of a great contemporary sports hero, Lance Armstrong. The speaker uses certain words and phrases to tell the chronology of his life. These are words and phrases such as the following:

> Lance Armstrong was born on September 18, 1971 . . .
> . . . when he was only 10 years old.
> When he turned 16, . . .
> By 1991, . . .
> . . . a few months away from his 25th birthday, . . .
> . . . shortly after his 25th birthday,
> Quite soon after, . . .
> . . . in 2004.

II. LISTENING

∩ A. Initial Listening

Now let's listen to a talk about Lance Armstrong. It may help you to concentrate on the talk if you close your eyes while you listen. Just relax and listen carefully.

🎧 B. Mental Rehearsal and Review of the Talk

Let's listen to the talk once again. This time, the narrative about Lance Armstrong will be given in message units. Please repeat each unit to yourself silently after you hear it. Remember, do not repeat the units out loud.

C. Consolidation

You will now hear the talk given once again. This time as you listen, take notes on what you hear.

III. POSTLISTENING

🎧 A. The Comprehension Check

1. Recognizing Information and Checking Accuracy

For questions 1–6 you will hear multiple-choice questions about the information presented in the talk. Listen to each question and decide whether (a), (b), (c), or (d) is the best answer to the question.

_____ 1. (a) 5
       (b) 10
       (c) 13
       (d) 25

_____ 2. (a) the Tour du Pont
       (b) the Iron Kids Triathlon
       (c) the Classico San Sebastion
       (d) the U.S. National Amateur Championship

_____ 3. (a) 16
       (b) 24
       (c) 25
       (d) 32

_____ 4. (a) almost 0%
       (b) almost 100%
       (c) less than 50-50
       (d) more than 50-50

_____ 5. (a) his mother
       (b) a French team
       (c) the U.S. Olympic team
       (d) the U.S. Postal Service Team

_____ 6. (a) *Cancer Survivor*
       (b) *Every Second Counts*
       (c) *Number One in the World*
       (d) *I Owe It All to My Mother*

For questions 7–10, you will hear statements about Lance Armstrong. If the statement is true, put a *T* on the line next to the number of the statement. If the statement you hear is false, put an *F* on the line and explain why the statement is false.

7. _____   8. _____   9. _____   10. _____

2. Using and Expanding on the Information in the Talk

a. Recapping the Information from Your Notes. Use your notes to recap the information you learned about the life and struggle of Lance Armstrong.

b. Expanding on the Information in the Talk. Discuss the following questions with a classmate:

1. Who are the two most important sports heroes in your country today? Why are they important?

2. Who are your heroes in life? Your father? Mother? Someone in sports? A historical figure? Explain your choice.

3. Do you agree with this statement: Lance Armstrong survived his cancer because he was rich and able to have the best medical treatment available. Why or why not?

∩ B. The Listening Expansion

Task 1.   **Filling in Information and Answering Questions**

Cycling is not only a popular sport, but an economical, efficient means of transportation for many people. You are going to listen to a short history of the bicycle. As you listen, follow along in your book. While you listen and read, fill in the missing information in the blank spaces.

History of the Bicycle

The precursor to the bicycle appeared in France in the _____. It was a little wooden horse with a fixed front wheel. Because the wheel was fixed, it could not be turned right or left. This little horse did not have any pedals, and the only way it could be maneuvered was by the rider pushing against the ground with his or her feet.

In _____ the German baron Karl von Drais replaced the fixed front wheel with one that could be steered. Now the wooden horse could be directed right or left. The rider still needed to push it with his or her feet on the ground.

The next development occurred in _____, when a Scottish blacksmith, Kirkpatrick MacMillan, designed the first bicycle-like machine with pedals and cranks. MacMillan called his machine a "velocipede" and rode it the 40 miles from his home to Glasgow, Scotland in only _____ hours.

In _____ Pierre Lallement applied for and received a U.S. patent for a machine that he called the "bisicle." Some people called it a "boneshaker" as it had steel-rimmed wooden wheels. The bicycle got more comfortable in _____ when rubber tires were introduced. _____ _____ _____ _____, the front wheels began to grow larger while the back wheels got smaller, and the first "highwheeler" was introduced in 1872. During the _____, bicycles enjoyed a boom—that is, a sudden growth in popularity. The highwheelers were very popular, especially among young men, as they could go very fast. However, they weren't very safe. Sitting high up towards the front of the bicycle and traveling very fast, the rider could be easily thrown over the front wheel if the bicycle hit a small bump in the road or if a dog ran in front of the bicycle. This type of accident gave rise to the expression "to do a header" as the rider often fell onto his head.

Fortunately, the "safety bicycle" was invented in _____. The safety bicycle had equal-sized wheels, a chain, and a sprocket-driven rear wheel. The rider was _____ sitting further back on the bicycle and in much less danger of "doing a header." More improvements _____ followed. Pneumatic tires—that is, tires with air in them— were invented in _____. Two- and three-speed hub gears came in the 1890s. The last major innovation, the derailleur gear, arrived in _____. No further significant changes were made until the 1970s. In the 1970s bicycles became more aerodynamic. That is, changes in design and use of lightweight but strong materials allowed bicycles to reduce the amount of air resistance they encountered and thus go faster. No doubt there will be further improvements in design and materials in the future.

CHECK YOUR ANSWERS ▶

Task 2.   **Listening to Identify Famous People**

Look at the names of the following famous people. Think about what you know about each person. Then listen to a series of brief biographies and match the number of each biography to the correct name. Are you ready to listen to the first biography? Listen carefully.

1. _____   a. Princess Diana

2. _____   b. Mother Teresa

3. _____   c. Marco Polo

4. _____   d. Ghengis Khan

5. _____   e. Alexander the Great

6. _____   f. Pele

7. _____   g. Cleopatra

CHECK YOUR ANSWERS ▶ 8. _____   h. Ibn Batuta

LISTENING FACTOIDS

#1 There are millions of bicycles in the world and the bicycle is the major means of transportation for millions of people. Listen to learn some scientific information about how energy–efficient the bicycle is.

#2 Professor Steve Jones, a geneticist, says that the invention of the bicycle is one of the three most important inventions in human history. Listen to find out what the other two inventions were and what the significance of each of the three inventions was.

Focus on:
Process

Process tells how to do something, how something works, or how something happens.

The Internet:
How It Works

I. PRELISTENING

A. Listening Preparation

Millions of people use the Internet everyday to send and receive e-mail messages, to find information on the World Wide Web, or to download files, such as games, music files or movie clips. What is the Internet and how does it work? How do e-mail messages get from your computer to the computer of the person you send them to? How do Web pages travel to your computer? How do files you download reach your computer?

B. Preview of Vocabulary and Sentences

to link together into a gigantic network to connect and form an extremely large network
- The Internet consists of millions of computers, all *linked together into a gigantic network*.

to equip with software to supply a program, or set of instructions, that tells the computer to perform some activity
- These computers are *equipped with* special communication *software*.

monthly charge an amount of money to be paid each month, usually for a service such as telephone service
- An Internet Service Provider (ISP) is a company that provides Internet service for a *monthly charge*.

in turn in correct order or sequence
- Local ISPs connect to larger ISPs, which *in turn* connect to even larger ISPs.

hierarchy a pyramid-like organizational structure such as found in businesses and the military, where the few at the top have the most power
- A *hierarchy* of networks is formed.

to break down to separate into parts or pieces
- The data, or information, in an e-mail message, a Web page, or a file is first *broken down* into tiny packets.

route a way to reach a place

destination the place that someone or something is going
- The router then decides the best *route* to send the packet on its way to its *destination*.

to imagine to form a mental picture
- *Imagine* that you want to send a friend a book, but you can send it only as postcards.

postal agent person who works for the post office or a mail service and who has the authority to make decisions
- Many *postal agents* may look at the addresses on the postcards in order to decide the best route to send them off on to reach their destination.

C. Rhetorical Listening Cues

In this talk, the speaker explains how the Internet works, that is, how information travels over the Internet. The speaker uses words and phrases to show the order, or sequence, of how information travels over the Internet. These are words such as *first, then, when, after*, and *finally*.

The speaker also uses an *analogy*, or comparison, to help explain the process. Some common analogies you might be familiar with are:

The heart is like a pump.
The Internet is like an information highway.
Learning to drive is like learning to ride a bicycle (once you learn, you never forget how).

In this lecture, the speaker compares how information travels through the Internet with how postcards are sent through the postal system.

II. LISTENING

∩ A. Initial Listening

Now let's listen to a talk about what the Internet is and how it works.

∩ B. Mental Rehearsal and Review of the Talk

Let's listen to the talk once more. This time the description of the Internet and how it works will be given in message units. Please repeat each of the sentences or phrases to yourself silently as you hear it spoken. Remember, do not repeat the units out loud.

∩ C. Consolidation

You will now hear the talk once again. This time as you listen, take notes on what you hear.

III. POSTLISTENING

∩ A. The Comprehension Check

1. Recognizing Information and Checking Accuracy

For questions 1–4, you will hear multiple-choice questions about the information presented in the talk. Listen to each question and decide whether (a), (b), (c), or (d) is the best answer to the question.

_____ 1. (a) hundreds of ISPs
         (b) tiny packets of information
         (c) individuals, organizations, and companies
         (d) a gigantic network of connected computers

_____ 2. (a) an ISP
         (b) a postal agent
         (c) a specialized computer
         (d) communication software

_____ 3. (a) a book
         (b) software
         (c) a network
         (d) its destination address

_____ 4. (a) postcard
         (b) postal agent
         (c) page of a book
         (d) packet of information

For questions 5–7, you will hear statements about the Internet and how it works. If the statement is true, put a T on the line next to the number of the statement. If the statement you hear is false, put an F on the line, and explain why the statement is false.

CHECK YOUR ANSWERS ▶   5. _____   6. _____   7. _____

2. Using and Expanding on the Information in the Talk

a. Recapping the Information from Your Notes.   Use your notes to recap the information you learned about how the information in e-mail messages, Web pages, and downloaded files travel over the Internet.

b. Expanding on the Information in the Talk.   Discuss with a classmate why you agree (or do not agree) with the following statements.

1. The Internet is the best place to find information on almost everything.

2. Information on the Internet is usually quite accurate.

3. The government needs to control the kind of information that can be on the Internet.

4. Every student should have a laptop computer and an Internet connection.

∩ B. The Listening Expansion

Task 1.   **Connecting the Processes**

Viruses, worms, Trojans! It seems that every week there is something in the news about these invaders that make your computer "sick."

These invaders often do very harmful things, such as delete files, access your personal data, or use your computer to attack other computers. Viruses can spread and infect other computers very quickly. It's possible for a virus to go around the world in minutes. There are several things you can do to protect your computer against these invaders, but one of the most important is to have good antivirus software. If you use the Internet at all, or if you ever borrow a disk from anyone, you almost certainly need to have antivirus software. Let's listen to a talk about how to choose the best antivirus software for you. Fill in the missing transitional cues.

Once you decide that you need good antivirus software, _____ _____ _____ to do is to see whether your computer already
                    (1)
has an antivirus program pre-installed. You can do this by going to Programs on your Start menu and looking for an antivirus software program. If you find there is an antivirus program already installed, _____
                                                                        (2)
check to see if it is activiated. _____ determine whether it is up to
                                   (3)
date. _____, consider whether it's the best software for your needs. If,
        (4)
_____ _____ this process, you decide you need to purchase antivirus
    (5)
software, here are _____ _____ you can follow.
                          (6)

_____, ask friends and colleagues for their recommendations.
    (7)
_____ _____, go to the Internet to read several reviews of antivirus
      (8)
software programs. You will see that there are some free antivirus software programs available to be downloaded. If one of them suits your needs, _____ your search may be over. If not, _____ _____
               (9)   (10)
many reviews, select a few software programs to consider purchasing. _____ _____ _____ is to test them if possible. Many
                      (11)
programs' Web sites allow you to download them for a trial period. _____ _____ _____, compare prices of these programs.
               (12)

_____ _____ all these steps, you should be ready to purchase
        (13)
your software. If your computer already has an antivirus software program, be sure to uninstall it _____ _____ your new software.
                                                        (14)
_____, install your new antivirus software following the manufac-
    (15)
turer's direction carefully. Keep in mind that antivirus software must be continuously updated to be effective.

Task 2.

A Dictation: How to Be a Courteous E-mail Correspondent

E-mail is a wonderful and inexpensive way to keep in touch with friends and family. Because e-mail is a newer way to communicate than regular mail or the telephone, not everybody knows how to be a courteous (that is, polite) e-mail correspondent. The speaker is going to dictate five simple, short rules. As you listen, write these rules on the lines below. After you have checked these rules with your teacher, please write one or two more rules that you think would be helpful. Then put number 1 next to the rule you think is most important, number 2 next to the next most important rule, etc.

a. _____

b. _____

c. _____

d. _____

e. _____

_____

CHECK YOUR ANSWERS ▶

_____

 LISTENING FACTOIDS

#1 When do you think people are more likely to lie—in phone conversations or in e-mails? Listen to an interesting study reported in *NewScientist.com* on February 12, 2004.

#2 Spam! What is it? Who likes it? Is it a serious problem? Listen.

Language:
How Children Acquire Theirs

I. PRELISTENING

A. Listening Preparation

How do babies communicate before they know how to speak any language? When do they begin to make language-like sounds? Are these first language-like sounds the same for all babies, or do babies from different language backgrounds make different sounds? At what age do they begin to say their first words? What does it mean that children's first sentences are "telegraphic"? What kinds of grammar mistakes do children make when learning their own language? You will learn the answers to these questions when you listen to the talk on how children acquire their language.

B. Preview of Vocabulary and Sentences

cooing noises soft and gentle sounds like the sounds a pigeon makes
- The first stage begins in a few weeks when they start to make *cooing noises* when they are happy.

to babble to make and play with meaningless sounds like "goo-goo-goo" and "da-da-da"
- Around four months of age babies begin *to babble.*

to invent words to create their own special words
- These first words are *words* that they *invent* for themselves; for example, a baby may say "baba" for the word "bottle," or "kiki" for "cat."

to acquire words to learn words
- In the next few months, the baby will *acquire* quite a few *words* and begin to use them to communicate with others.

telegraphic in the style of a telegram, that is, expressed in as short a way as possible

essential basic, necessary, required
- This language is often called *telegraphic* speech because the baby omits all except the most *essential* words.

to overgeneralize to use a rule too freely; to use a rule where it doesn't fit
- They also begin to *overgeneralize* these grammar rules and make a lot of grammar mistakes.

C. Rhetorical Listening Cues

In this talk the speaker discusses how children acquire language. The speaker uses certain words and phrases to show the order, or the sequence, of the process. These are words and phrases such as the following:

As soon as . . .
At first, . . .
The first stage . . .
The next stage . . .

II. LISTENING

🎧 A. Initial Listening

Now let's listen to a talk about how children acquire language. It may help you to concentrate on the talk if you close your eyes while you listen. Just relax and listen carefully.

🎧 B. Mental Rehearsal and Review of the Talk

Let's listen to the talk once more. This time the description of how children acquire language will be given in message units. Please repeat each of the sentences or phrases to yourself silently as you hear it spoken. Remember, do not repeat the units out loud.

🎧 C. Consolidation

You will hear the talk given once again. This time, as you listen, take notes on what you hear.

III. POSTLISTENING

🎧 A. The Comprehension Check

1. Recognizing Information and Checking Accuracy

For questions 1–3 you will hear multiple-choice questions about the information presented in the talk. Listen to each question and decide whether (a), (b), (c), or (d) is the best answer to the question.

_____ 1. at_____
   (a) birth
   (b) 4 months
   (c) 10 months
   (d) 18 months

_____ 2. (a) "kiki"
   (b) "Daddy up"
   (c) "I went home."
   (d) "I goed sleep."

_____ 3. (a) 10–12 months
   (b) 18–24 months
   (c) 2–3 years
   (d) 7–8 years

For question 4–7 you will hear statements about how children acquire language. If the statement is true, put a *T* on the line next to the number of the statement. If the statement you hear is false, put an *F* on the line.

CHECK YOUR ANSWERS ▶   4. _____   5. _____   6. _____   7. _____

2. Using and Expanding on the Information in the Talk

a. Recapping Information from Your Notes. Use your notes to recap the information you learned about how children acquire language. Present the information to the class or to one of your classmates.

b. Expanding on the Information in the Talk. Discuss with a classmate why you agree (or do not agree) with the following statements:

1. It is very confusing for a baby to have to learn two languages at the same time, so parents who speak two different languages should agree to speak only one language to the child.

2. It's important for parents to talk to their babies a lot to help them learn their language.

3. Some language are more difficult for babies to learn than other languages.

4. It's easy for a baby to learn his or her language, but it's hard work for an adult to learn a second language.

5. Babies would not learn to talk if nobody spoke to them.

6. All people who live in a country should be able to speak at least one common language.

7. It would be better if everybody in the world spoke the same language.

8. Some languages are better for science, some for poetry, and others for romance and love.

Task 1.   **Solving a Word Problem**

You are going to listen to a problem that needs to be solved. Look at the picture as you listen to the problem. After you listen to the problem, discuss it with a partner to be sure you both understand the nature of the problem. Then work together to try to solve the problem. Now, listen to the problem.

When you think you have a solution, find another pair of students who have also solved the problem. Take turns explaining the process you used in finding a solution to the problem. For example, "First, we tried . . . . After that, we . . . . Next, we . . . . Finally, ..."

CHECK YOUR ANSWERS ▶

Task 2.

Explaining Steps in Problem Solving

You will need a piece of paper and three coins of different sizes to solve the following problem. When you are ready, listen to the problem. When you have listened to the problem, discuss the problem with a partner to be sure you both understand the nature of the problem. Then work on the problem until you solve it.

After you have solved the problem, write out the steps that must be followed in order to solve this problem. Begin this way, "First, move the (name of coin) to . . . . Next, ..." Continue until you have listed every step necessary to solve the problem.

CHECK YOUR ANSWERS ▶

#1 Listen to the story of an ancient experiment to discover what language children would speak if they never heard anyone speaking their language.

#2 Who uses baby talk? Listen and learn why both adults and babies use baby talk. Also listen to find out what sounds babies around the world make as they begin to speak their language.

Hydroponic Aquaculture:
How One System Works

I. PRELISTENING

A. Listening Preparation

According to a recent article in the *Arizona Daily Star* newspaper, there are many countries and places in the world that lack three essential commodities: vegetables, fish, and water. Today, however, scientists have developed a simple but effective method of producing fish and vegetables in water (rather than soil) using hydroponic aquaculture. How do scientists do this? First, they collect rainwater in a large tank. Then they raise fish in the rainwater they collected, and, finally, they grow vegetables on the waste from the fish raised in the rainwater. How can fish and vegetables be raised in an aquaculture (or hydroponic) environment? Let me tell you how one hydroponic process functions. I'll describe for you an aquaculture experiment that raises fish and vegetables on the Island of St. Croix in the Virgin Islands.

B. Preview of Vocabulary and Sentences

substances the materials something is made of
- The growing of plants without soil has developed from experiments carried out to determine what *substances* (like soil and water) make plants grow.

precede to go before in time
- Scientists believe hydroponic growing actually *preceded* soil growing.

tray a raised, flat surface that is used to hold items (such as plants)
- Just above the 100-foot long tanks of water, lettuce plants are suspended on *trays*.

to soak up (to absorb) to take in and make a part of itself

nutrient an element in food that is needed by people, animals, and plants for life and growth
- The plants *soak up* or *absorb* the nitrates and other *nutrients* in the water.

pump a machine that is used to move water and other liquids or a gas from one place to another place
- A *pump* is used to cycle the water back up to the 3,000-gallon fish tank.

profitable money making
- A commercial company would need to have several tanks in order to make the process *profitable*.

C. Rhetorical Listening Cues

In this talk the speaker discusses how one system of hydroponic aquaculture works. The speaker uses certain words and phrases to show the order, or the sequence, of the process described. These are words and phrases such as the following:

> To start with . . .
> Once the tank is filled, . . .
> First, . . .
> Subsequently, . . .
> The next step in the process, . . .
> After it is filtered, . . .
> It is now necessary to . . .
> The nitrates are then used to . . .
> So what happens next?
> And then the hydroponic process starts all over again.

II. LISTENING

A. Initial Listening

Now let's listen to a talk about a hydroponic experiment to raise fish and lettuce plants. Look at the illustration of the process as you listen to the talk.

B. Mental Rehearsal and Review of the Talk

Let's listen to the talk once more. This time the description of the aquaculture process will be given in message units. Please repeat each of the sentences or phrases to yourself silently as you hear it spoken. Remember, do not repeat the units out loud.

C. Consolidation

You will hear the talk given once again. This time as you listen, take notes on what you hear.

III. POSTLISTENING

A. The Comprehension Check

1. Recognizing Information and Checking Accuracy

For questions 1–5, you will hear multiple-choice questions about the information presented in the talk. Listen to each question and decide whether (a), (b), (c), or (d) is the best answer to the question.

_____ 1. (a) As old as the pyramids.
         (b) More years than you think.
         (c) As ancient as the city of Babylon.
         (d) All of the above.

_____ 2. (a) Babylon
         (b) Egypt
         (c) India
         (d) Kashmir

_____ 3. (a) bacteria
         (b) nitrates
         (c) filtering
         (d) gravity

_____ 4. (a) bacteria
         (b) nitrates
         (c) filtering
         (d) gravity

_____ 5. (a) 1,000
         (b) 3,000
         (c) 10,000
         (d) 25,000

For questions 6–10, you will hear statements about hydroponic aquaculture. If the statement is true, put a _T_ on the line next to the number of the statement. If the statement is false, put an _F_ on the line and explain why the statement is false.

CHECK YOUR ANSWERS ▶

6. _____   7. _____   8. _____   9. _____   10. _____

2. Using and Expanding on the Information in the Talk

a. Recapping the Information from Your Notes. Use your notes to recap the information you learned about the hydroponic system of growing lettuce. Present the information to the class or to one of your classmates.

b. Expanding on the Information in the Talk. Discuss with a classmate why you agree (or do not agree) with the following statements:

1. Hydoponic aquaculture would be a cost-effective and efficient method of growing food in my country.

2. Many things could go wrong with hydroponic aquaculture.

3. Developing countries would benefit more using aquaculture than would developed countries.

4. I would prefer to eat vegetables grown in soil than in the hydroponic environment.

5. Some people eat to live; others live to eat. I live to eat.

6. If the following foods were prepared and served for dinner at a friend's house, I would eat:

   horse meat
   snake meat
   grasshoppers and crickets
   raw fish
   roast dog
   monkey meat
   pork
   camel meat
   kangaroo meat
   elephant meat
   octopus
   the eyes of an animal
   the brains of an animal
   the heart and intestine of an animal
   mushrooms a friend found in the woods near his house

Task 1.   **Listening to Identify Steps**

You are going to listen to steps that can be followed to achieve a yoga position. First look at the seven pictures below. These pictures are the steps necessary to do the yoga exercise. However, they are not in the correct order. You must listen carefully and number the pictures. (Notice that two of the pictures are the same, but you will need both of them in order to complete the steps.)

Now that you have finished putting the pictures in the correct order, you could try out the yoga exercise. Don't worry if you can't do it perfectly. Just move as far as is comfortable for you. Never do anything that hurts or makes you uncomfortable.

CHECK YOUR ANSWERS ▶

Task 2.   **Taking Your Pulse**

People who exercise vigorously, for example, people who run or ride a bicycle, are often interested in knowing what their pulse rate is before and after they exercise. Taking your pulse is easy. Listen to the steps. You may want to take brief notes.

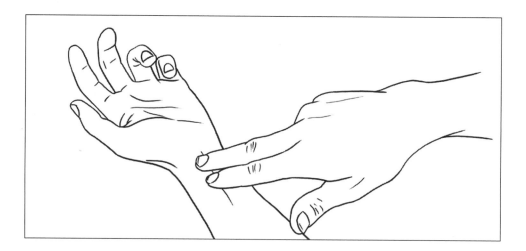

Practice explaining these steps to a partner. Then take your pulse and write the number here. Pulse Rate _____

#1 Just listen to this fact about the jackfruit.

#2 Can we grow plants in regions with poor soil or no soil? Listen to find out how the Aztecs of Central America did hydroponic gardening long ago.

Focus on:
Classification/Definition

Classification is a way of putting people, places, things, or ideas into groups or classes. All of the items in one class have something in common. The classes are separate and complete, and are often organized by physical features or uses. Definition is a way of first describing how something is a member of a general class (genus) and then how the subject is different from all others of that class.

A Tidal Wave:

What Is It? What Causes It?
How Can We Predict it?

I. PRELISTENING

A. Listening Preparation

Tidal waves are one of the great forces of nature. Tidal waves can be very dangerous to people. They have caused a lot of destruction to property, and they have killed many people. What exactly is a tidal wave? What causes a tidal wave? How can we predict when a tidal wave will strike? Do you know the answers to these questions? Listen and find out.

B. Preview of Vocabulary Sentences

destructive damaging; causing ruin

to rush to move forward very quickly; to speed
- A tidal wave is a very large and *destructive* wall of water that *rushes* in from the ocean toward the shore.

storms heavy, windy rainfalls or snowfalls
- Do you know that tidal waves are not caused by *storms*?

to shift to change position
- When a seaquake takes place at the bottom of the ocean, the ocean floor shakes and trembles and sometimes *shifts*.

to predict to tell in advance; to foretell
- Today scientists can *predict* when a tidal wave will hit land.

to warn to advise of coming danger
- It is possible to *warn* people that a tidal wave is coming.

C. Rhetorical Listening Clues

In this talk you will hear several definitions given. In other words, the speaker will explain the meanings of some of the words or expressions. Sometimes the speaker will explain an expression by telling you what it is. For example, you will hear, "A tidal wave is a very large and very destructive wave that rushes in from the ocean like a huge tide." And sometimes you will hear the speaker explain a word or expression by telling you what it is not. For example, you will hear, "Tidal waves are not true tides." This is an example of a *negative* definition. Sometimes the speaker will give you a synonym for a word. Sometimes the speaker will explain a word by breaking it down into its parts. For example, the word "seaquake" is made up of two words: "sea" and "quake." The speaker will explain the meaning of *both* words. You will hear the speaker define the following word or words: "tidal wave," "true tide," "seaquake," "to quake," and "seismograph."

II. LISTENING

🎧 *A. Initial Listening*

> Now let's listen to a talk about what a tidal wave is, what causes a tidal wave, and how a tidal wave can be predicted by scientists. It may help you to concentrate on the talk if you close your eyes while you listen. Just relax and listen carefully.

🎧 *B. Mental Rehearsal and Review of the Talk*

> All right. Let's listen to the talk once again. This time, the talk will be given in message units. Please repeat each unit to yourself silently after you hear it. Remember, don't say the units out loud.

🎧 *C. Consolidation*

> You will hear the talk given once again. This time as you listen, take notes on what you hear.

III. POSTLISTENING

🎧 *A. The Comprehension Check*

1. Recognizing Information and Checking Accuracy

Are you ready for a quiz on the story? Column A contains six blank lines. Column B lists some words and phrases from the story. Look over the information in Column B. Here's what you have to do. First, you will listen to a statement. Then you should look at the choices listed in Column B. Match the correct choice with the statement you hear. For example: Look at 1 in Column A. Statement 1 is "In Japanese it means 'storm wave'." The correct match to the statement, "In Japanese it means 'storm wave'" is choice *a—tsunami*. Put the letter *a* on line 1. Are you ready to do some more? We'll start with statement 2.

Column A	Column B
_____ 1.	**a.** tsunami
_____ 2.	**b.** seaquake
_____ 3.	**c.** scientists
_____ 4.	**d.** tidal wave
_____ 5.	**e.** ocean floor
_____ 6.	**f.** a seismograph
	g. earthquake
	h. Richter scale

CHECK YOUR ANSWERS ▶

2. Using and Expanding on the Information in the Talk

a. Recapping the Information from Your Notes. Use your notes to recap the information you learned about *tsunamis*. Present the information to the class or to one of your classmates.

b. Expanding on the Information in the Talk. Discuss with a classmate the following issues:

1. Natural disasters threaten many populations throughout the world, but natural disasters are not the only or most frightening disasters people face. Diseases like AIDS might put an end to humankind one day. Natural disasters like *tsunamis* cannot be prevented, but we can do something about the spread of AIDS. What can we do to prevent the spread of AIDS, tuberculosis, and the other contagious diseases that are on the increase?

2. Life expectancy has increased in most countries of the world. Why?

3. How long would you like to live? Why?

4. Many countries still have very low life expectancy. Why? What can be done to help increase the life expectancy of people in these countries?

5. The worst kind of natural disaster is _____ because _____.

Task 1.   **Filling In Information and Answering Questions**

In this exercise you will complete a crossword puzzle using words from the story. Some of the words will be written across and some of the words will be written down. When two words meet or cross each other, they will share a common letter. For example, number 1 across and number 1 down both begin with the same letter. Let's do number 1 across together. Are you ready? Number 1 across: It's a word with 11 letters. It's an instrument that records information about an earthquake. The word is "seismograph." Write the word "seismograph" beginning in box 1 and continuing across to box 11. Seismograph is spelled s-e-i-s-m-o-g-r-a-p-h. Are you ready to complete the puzzle? I will tell you how many letters each word has and give you a definition of the word. You may not know how to spell each word. Just do your best. Let's begin.

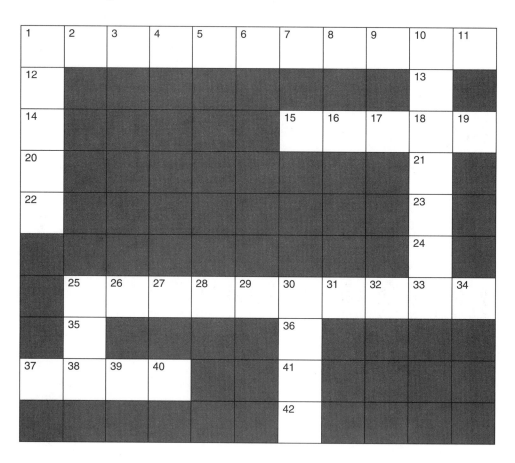

CHECK YOUR ANSWERS ▶

Task 2.　　　**Catching and Correcting Mistakes in Information**

In this exercise you will listen to a brief news report about a tidal wave that struck Japan several years ago. Like all news reports, this report is full of factual information. Factual information contains the names of places, dates, numbers, or happenings. After you listen to the report, you will read five statements about the tidal wave. You will check the accuracy of some statements made about the event, about the tidal wave, by catching the errors and correcting the sentences.

Now listen carefully to the news report of the event that happened on May 26, 1983, in northwestern Japan. Ready?

Now read the following statements related to the news report you just heard. Each statement contains one error or one incorrect piece of information. Correct the mistake by restating the sentence correctly. For example, you will read: "An earthquake struck the northeastern coast of Japan." You will say: "An earthquake struck the *northwestern* coast of Japan."

1. Fifteen people were caught in the tidal wave.

2. The tidal wave hit the coast an hour after the earthquake.

3. A 20-foot-high wave struck the beach.

4. The quake caused widespread destruction of beaches.

5. The president of the United States declared a state of emergency.

CHECK YOUR ANSWERS ▶

LISTENING FACTOIDS

#1 On August 27, 1883, the volcanic island of Krakatoa blew up. Some 36,000 people were killed by the *tsunamis* that followed the eruption and the earthquake, but do you know that the largest wave known was not a *tsunami*? Listen.

#2 When a *tsunami* occurs, it can create a deadly wall of water that rises more than 100 feet (30 meters) high. Listen to how fast a *tsunami* can travel.

Levels of Language Usage:
Formal and Informal

I. PRELISTENING

A. Listening Preparation

Have you ever said something in English and had someone look at you in surprise, laugh at you, or even look at you with uncomprehending eyes? You might have thought you had made a mistake in English grammar or used the wrong word or phrase. However, maybe you didn't make a grammar or vocabulary mistake. It's possible to use English that is appropriate in one situation but that is not appropriate in another situation. Learning a language means not only learning a new grammar and a lot of new words and phrases, but it also means learning how to choose appropriate words and expressions for the situation you are in.

B. Preview of Vocabulary and Sentences

reference books books where one can look up factual information, usually arranged by alphabet, topics, or dates
- Formal written language is found in *reference books* such as encyclopedias.

ceremonies formal activities associated with special occasions
- You will hear formal language at *ceremonies* such as graduations.

to tend to to be likely or inclined to
- We *tend to* use spoken formal language in conversations with persons we don't know well.

colleagues fellow workers in a profession; professional equals
- Informal language is used in conversation with *colleagues*, family, and friends.

diaries daily written records of what we do, think, or feel, usually kept private
- Informal language is also used when we write personal notes or letters to close friends, as well as in *diaries*.

in authority in a position of power over other people
- I would use formal English with a stranger or someone *in authority*.

teammates fellow members of a team, usually a sports team
- Classmates, *teammates*, family members, friends, etc., will generally speak in an informal fashion.

interacting entering into relationships, social or professional
- The difference between formal and informal usage can be learned by observing and *interacting* with native speakers.

C. Rhetorical Listening Cues

In this talk the speaker classifies Standard English into two broad categories, or levels, of language usage: formal English and informal English. The speaker gives examples of where each of these levels of English should be used and then gives examples of sentences in both formal and informal English.

II. LISTENING

A. Initial Listening

Now let's listen to a talk about formal and informal levels of English usage. It may help you to concentrate on the talk if you close your eyes while you listen. Just relax and listen carefully.

B. Mental Rehearsal and Review of the Talk

Let's listen to the talk once more. This time the description of the levels of English usage will be given in message units. Please repeat each of the sentences or phrases to yourself silently as you hear it spoken. Remember, do not repeat the units out loud.

C. Consolidation

You will hear the talk given once again. This time as you listen, take notes on what you hear.

III. POSTLISTENING

A. The Comprehension Check

1. Recognizing Information and Checking Accuracy

For questions 1–4 you will hear multiple-choice questions about the information presented in the talk. Listen to each question and decide whether (a), (b), (c), or (d) is the best answer to the question.

_____ 1. (a) diaries
    (b) compositions
    (c) personal notes
    (d) letters to friends

_____ 2. (a) family
    (b) friends
    (c) teammates
    (d) a, b, & c

_____ 3. (a) Salt, please.
    (b) Pass the salt.
    (c) Pass the salt, please.
    (d) Could you please pass the salt?

_____ 4. (a) I enjoy music.
    (b) I saw the cops.
    (c) I like Greek food.
    (d) None of the above.

For questions 5–8 you will hear statements about levels of English usage. If the statement is true, put a T on the line next to the number of the statement. If the statement you hear is false, put an F on the line, and explain why the statement is false.

CHECK YOUR ANSWERS ▶

5. ____   6. ____   7. ____   8. ____

2. Using and Expanding on the Information in the Talk

a. Recapping the Information from Your Notes. Use your notes to recap the information you learned about formal and informal levels of English usage. Present the information to the class or to one of your classmates.

b. Expanding on the Information in the Talk. Discuss with a classmate why you agree (or do not agree) with the following statements:

1. It would be better to speak formal English in all situations.

2. It's too difficult for second language learners to learn the difference between formal and informal English. Only native speakers can learn the difference.

3. If a person is not sure which language level to use, it's better to use formal English instead of informal English.

4. Children should be spoken to in informal language.

5. The way a person speaks tells you a lot about that person.

6. English teachers do not teach students how to use informal English, and this causes problems for second language learners.

Task 1. **Labeling the Parts of an Ancient Calculator**

You are going to hear about an ancient calculator called an *abacus*. You will hear a definition of what an abacus is and then will label its parts.

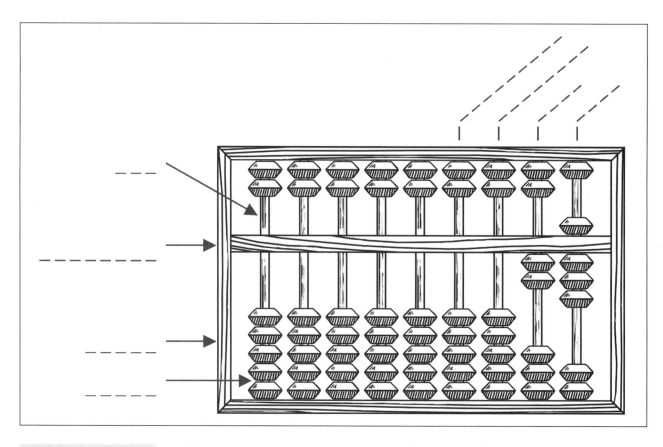

CHECK YOUR ANSWERS ▶ If there is someone in your class who knows how to use an abacus, ask your classmate to do a few arithmetic problems to show you how quickly and accurately arithmetic calculations can be made on an abacus.

Task 2.   **Labeling the Parts of a Modern Calculator**

Modern calculators will do a lot more than the ancient abacus. The abacus is a manual calculator, while modern calculators are electronic. These modern electronic calculators still do the same arithmetic computations that the abacus does, but they also do a variety of other calculations. Today you will label the parts of this fairly simple, modern electronic calculator.

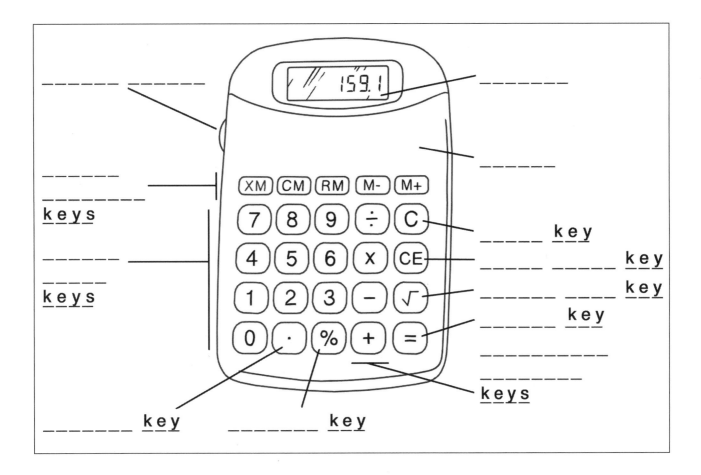

CHECK YOUR ANSWERS ▶

If there is anyone in your class who knows how to use the memory keys, ask your classmate to explain the purpose and use of these keys.

#1 A good English-English dictionary can be helpful in determining the level of usage of words as well as help you with spelling, pronunciation, and the meanings of words. For example, many dictionaries will tell you if a word is *informal*. Listen to a short talk about the very long time it can take to prepare a comprehensive dictionary.

#2 Slang is very informal language. Sometimes slang can be rude or vulgar, but often slang is simply words or expressions used by certain groups of people, for example, college students. The use of slang is also often generational. Listen to learn about the slang expressions, *swell*, *groovy*, and *cool* and how they have been used by different generations.

Power:
The Kinds People Use and Abuse

I. PRELISTENING

A. Listening Preparation

What is *power*? When you think of power, what do you think of? Money? Strength? Politics? The social psychologist Edwards defines power as *the ability to determine or to change the actions of other people.* What kinds of power do people use to influence the actions or *behavior* of other people? According to Edwards, they use five basic kinds of power: (1) information power; (2) referent power; (3) legitimate power; (4) expert power; and (5) reward and coercive (or punishment) power. In this talk, I will briefly describe each of these five classifications of power, and I'll give you some examples to illustrate a few of the types.

On the other hand, Edwards also says that a feeling of powerlessness is one of the most *disturbing* of human *emotions*—a feeling to be avoided at all costs.

B. Preview of Vocabulary and Sentences

a disturbing emotion a strong feeling that destroys a person's peace of mind
- On the other hand, he also says that a feeling of powerlessness is one of the most *disturbing* of human *emotions*—a feeling to be avoided at all costs.

behavior the way a person acts day after day or at any one time
- Psychologists define power as the ability to determine, or to change the actions or *behavior* of other people.

to manipulate other people to control other people in unfair or dishonest ways

for evil purposes for reasons that are bad or harmful to a person
- Psychologists are trying to understand how people *manipulate other people* for good and *evil purposes.*

to be in a position of power to have the authority to control or direct the actions of other people
- The person who has information that other people want and need, but do not have, is in *a position of power.*

own sense of power a person's feeling of personal control and influence over other people and events
- Most people like to receive and have information. Having information increases a person's *sense of power.*

accuracy correctness
- Many readers do not question the *accuracy* of the reports about world events they read in the newspapers.

to identify with a person to admire and to feel similar to a person
- If you *identify with another person,* that person has power over you and can influence your actions and behavior.

to imitate to try to act the way certain other people act and behave
- Many people *imitate* and are controlled by the people they identify with.

to commit suicide to kill oneself
- In the 1970s in Jonestown, Guyana, more than 900 people *committed suicide* when their religious leader Jim Jones told them to kill themselves.

Waco, Texas a small city in central Texas, in the United States
- More recently, a man named David Koresh controlled the lives and destinies of a small community of men, women, and children in *Waco, Texas.*

a civilian a person who is not in the army, police, etc.

a guard a person who protects someone or something from danger.

- In this experiment, a researcher asked people on the street to move away from a bus stop. When he was dressed as *a civilian*, few people moved away from the bus stop. When the researcher was dressed as *a guard*, most people moved away from the bus stop.

to be impressed by to have strong positive feelings about

- Most people *are impressed by* the skills or knowledge of experts.

a chance for gain an opportunity to benefit or be helped

- Giving a reward will change people's behavior because it offers people *a chance for gain*.

C. Rhetorical Listening Cues

In this talk, the speaker classifies various kinds of power. She begins by defining power, and she then goes on to discuss the different types of power. She uses words and phrases which indicate that she is classifying the various kinds of power, and is giving the order or sequence in which they are being discussed; she uses words such as "classify," "is classified," and expressions such as "the first type of power," "the third kind," and so forth.

II. LISTENING

A. Initial Listening

Now listen to a talk about the basic forms of power. It may help you to concentrate on the talk if you close your eyes while you listen. Just relax and listen carefully.

B. Mental Rehearsal and Review of the Talk

Let's listen to the talk once more. This time the classification of the various kinds of power will be given in message units. Please repeat each of the sentences or phrases to yourself silently as you hear it spoken. Remember, do not repeat the units out loud.

C. Consolidation

You will hear the talk given once again. This time as you listen, take notes on what you hear.

III. POSTLISTENING

A. The Comprehension Check

1. Recognizing Information and Checking Accuracy

For questions 1–4, you will hear multiple-choice questions about the information presented in the talk. Listen to each question and decide whether (a), (b), (c), or (d) is the best answer to the question.

_____ **1.** (a) reward
      (b) referent
      (c) legitimate
      (d) information

_____ **3.** (a) coercive
      (b) referent
      (c) legitimate
      (d) information

_____ **2.** (a) reward
      (b) referent
      (c) legitimate
      (d) information

_____ **4.** (a) expert
      (b) referent
      (c) legitimate
      (d) information

For questions 5–10, you will hear statements about various ideas. If the speaker mentioned the idea in the talk, put a check in the box "*I heard this idea in the talk.*" If, however, the idea was not mentioned in the talk, but you could infer the idea from the information given in the talk, put a check in the box, "*I didn't hear this idea but can infer it from the information given.*" Finally, if the idea you hear was not mentioned, and could not be inferred from the talk, check the box "*I did not hear this idea in the talk and cannot infer it from the information given.*"

	I heard this idea in the talk	I didn't hear this idea but can infer it from the information given	I did not hear this idea in the talk and cannot infer it from the information given
5.			
6.			
7.			
8.			
9.			
10.			

CHECK YOUR ANSWERS ▶

Now, you create four statements about the talk. Ask a classmate to listen as you say the statements and then to complete the chart.

	I heard this idea in the talk	I didn't hear this idea but can infer it from the information given	I did not hear this idea in the talk and cannot infer it from the information given
11.			
12.			
13.			
14.			

CHECK YOUR ANSWERS ▶

2. Using and Expanding on the Information in the Talk

a. Recapping the Information from Your Notes. Use your notes to recap the information you learned about the five basic kinds of power. Present the information to the class or to one of your classmates.

b. Expanding on the Information in the Talk. Discuss with a classmate why you agree (or do not agree) with the following statements:

1. To some people, power is a game in which winners are powerful, and losers are powerless.

2. There's a saying, "It's a man's world." Because it's a man's world, men have and use power, and women have little or no power.

3. Winning a war is the major sign of the power of a country.

4. Referent power is useful to rock stars and movie stars, generals in the army, religious leaders, and parents.

5. There are more than five basic kinds of power.

6. Information power is the most effective type of power.

7. Governments that use coercive power over their people generally use the coercive power for good purposes.

8. According to Ralph Waldo Emerson, "You shall have joy or you shall have power, said God; you shall not have both." Would you prefer to have joy or power? Or something else?

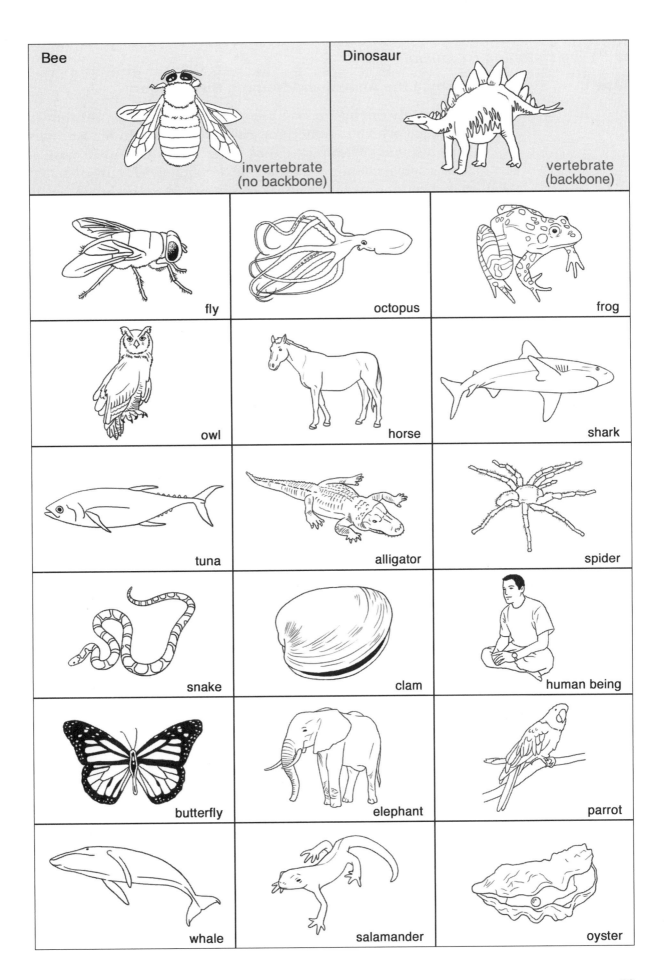

Bee	Dinosaur
invertebrate (no backbone)	vertebrate (backbone)

fly	octopus	frog
owl	horse	shark
tuna	alligator	spider
snake	clam	human being
butterfly	elephant	parrot
whale	salamander	oyster

B. The Listening Expansion

Task 1.   **Naming the Animal and Naming the Category**

All animals can be grouped according to whether or not they have a backbone, which is sometimes called a spinal column. Animals that have a spinal column are called "vertebrates." Animals that do not have a spinal column are called "invertebrates." A human being has a spinal column so she or he is classed as a "vertebrate." A bee has no spinal column. It is classed as an "invertebrate."

In this exercise you will listen to a description of a vertebrate animal or an invertebrate animal. You must first identify the animal described, and then you must categorize the animal as vertebrate or invertebrate by underlining the term "vertebrate" or "invertebrate."

Let's do 1 together. Listen to the following description. Look at the pictures of the animals on page 59.

1. Its a(n) _____. It's classed as a vertebrate/ invertebrate.

2. Its a(n) _____. It's categorized as a vertebrate/ invertebrate.

3. Its a(n) _____. It's designated as a vertebrate/ invertebrate.

4. Its a(n) _____. It's typed as a vertebrate/ invertebrate.

5. Its a(n) _____. It's classified as a vertebrate/ invertebrate.

6. Its a(n) _____. It's classed as a vertebrate/ invertebrate.

7. Its a(n) _____. It's categorized as a vertebrate/ invertebrate.

CHECK YOUR ANSWERS ▶

Task 2.   **The Five Categories of Vertebrates: Placing the Animal in the Category**

All vertebrate animals are divided into five general categories: mammals, fish, birds, reptiles, and amphibians. In this exercise, you will listen to and read definitions of each vertebrate category. After all the definitions have been given, you will use the information you heard to identify members of each category. Now follow along as the speaker explains what a mammal is. Listen carefully. The explanation is very general.

1. A *mammal* is a warm-blooded vertebrate that feeds its young with milk from the mother's body.

2. A *bird* is a warm-blooded vertebrate that has feathers and two feet. Instead of arms, a bird has wings.

3. A *fish* is a cold-blooded vertebrate that lives its entire life in water. It has fins instead of arms or feet. It gets oxygen from the water, not air.

4. A *reptile* is a cold-blooded vertebrate that crawls or moves on its stomach or on small short legs. Reptile babies hatch from eggs with shells.

5. An *amphibian* is a cold-blooded vertebrate that starts its life in water. Later, an amphibian develops lungs to breathe air. Then it can live on land.

Now you know the five categories of vertebrate animals. You will now hear the name of an animal. It may be a mammal, a bird, a fish, a reptile, or an amphibian. Listen for the name of the animal, and then write the name you hear on the blank line next to the correct number. Then write the category that the animal belongs to. For help, look at the pictures of the animals on page 59.

Animal	Category
1. _____	_____
2. _____	_____
3. _____	_____
4. _____	_____
5. _____	_____
6. _____	_____
7. _____	_____
8. _____	_____
9. _____	_____

CHECK YOUR ANSWERS ▶

| 10. _____ | _____ |

LISTENING FACTOIDS

#1 Listen to this fact about a king who was so powerful he was afraid someone would try to poison him.

#2 Now listen to another fact about an ancient society where powerful women ruled the land.

Focus on:
Comparison/Contrast

Comparison/contrast is a way of showing how people, places, things, ideas, or events are similar or different. Comparison describes the similarities between two or more things. Contrast describes the differences.

Asian and African Elephants:
Similarities and Differences

I. PRELISTENING

A. Listening Preparation

Elephants are fascinating animals. Almost everyone has seen an elephant in a zoo, in a circus, or, at least, in a picture. Tell me, what do you think of when you hear the word "elephant"? Do you know that there are two kinds of elephants? There's the African elephant and there's the Asian, or Indian, elephant. The African and the Asian elephants are alike, but they are also different in many ways. First, let's find out how they are similar, and then let's learn about how they are different. In other words, we are going to compare the African and the Asian elephants to see how they are alike. Then we are going to contrast these elephants to see how the African and the Asian elephants differ from one another.

B. Preview of Vocabulary and Sentences

enormous very large; huge; gigantic
- Elephants are really *enormous* animals.

trunks the long, round, muscular noses of elephants
- Both animals have long noses, called *trunks*.

to train to teach; to instruct
- Both animals can be *trained* to do heavy work.

trick a clever act, intended to amuse or puzzle
- Elephants can also be trained to do *tricks* to entertain people.

temperament personality; disposition; character
- The last big difference between the elephants is their *temperament*.

C. Rhetorical Listening Cues

In this talk the speaker compares and contrasts elephants. The speaker uses words that show similarity, words like "both" and "similarly." You will also hear words and phrases that show differences, words or phrases like "on the other hand," "in contrast," "but," "bigger than," and "more difficult than." These cues will tell you whether the speaker is comparing or contrasting two things—in this case two *big* animals.

II. LISTENING

🎧 A. Initial Listening

Now let's listen to a talk about the similarities and differences between Asian and African elephants. It may help you to concentrate on the talk if you close your eyes while you listen. Just relax and listen carefully.

🎧 B. Mental Rehearsal and Review of the Talk

All right. Let's listen to the talk once again. This time, the talk will be given in message units. Please repeat each unit to yourself silently after you hear it. Remember, don't say the units out loud.

🎧 C. Consolidation

You will hear the talk given once again. This time as you listen, take notes on what you hear.

III. POSTLISTENING

🎧 A. The Comprehension Check

1. Recognizing Information and Checking Accuracy

For questions 1–5 you will hear multiple-choice questions about the information presented in the talk. Listen to each question and decide whether (a), (b), (c), or (d) is the best answer to the question.

_____ 1. It's the elephant's _____.
   (a) ear
   (b) nose
   (c) tooth
   (d) tusk

_____ 2. (a) African elephants
   (b) Asian elephants
   (c) both of the above
   (d) neither of the above

_____ 3. _____ pounds
   (a) 7,000 to 12,000
   (b) 8,000 to 10,000
   (c) 12,000 to 14,000
   (d) 18,000 to 20,000

_____ 4. It is _____.
   (a) larger and lighter
   (b) heavier and larger
   (c) lighter and smaller
   (d) smaller and heavier

_____ 5. Both _____.
   (a) weigh the same
   (b) are similar in size
   (c) have a similar color
   (d) can learn tricks to entertain people

For questions 6–10, you will hear five statements about ideas. If the speaker mentioned the idea in the talk, put a check in the box "*I heard this idea in the talk.*" If, however, the idea was not mentioned in the talk, but you could *infer* the idea from the information given in the talk, put a check in the box, "*I didn't hear this idea but can infer it from the information given.*" Finally, if the idea you hear was not mentioned, and could not be inferred from the talk, check the box "*I did not hear this idea in the talk and cannot infer it from the information given.*"

	I heard this idea in the talk	I didn't hear this idea but can infer it from the information given	I did not hear this idea in the talk and cannot infer it from the information given
6.			
7.			
8.			
9.			
10.			

CHECK YOUR ANSWERS ▶

Now, you create four statements about the talk yourself. Ask a classmate to listen to the statements and to complete the chart below.

	I heard this idea in the talk	I didn't hear this idea but can infer it from the information given	I did not hear this idea in the talk and cannot infer it from the information given
11.			
12.			
13.			
14.			

CHECK YOUR ANSWERS ▶

2. Using and Expanding on the Information in the Talk

a. Recapping the Information from Your Notes.   Use your notes to recap the information you learned about African and Asian elephants. Present the information to the class or to one of your classmates.

b. Expanding on the Information in the Talk.   Discuss the following questions with a classmate:

1. What are the most important working animals in your country? What kind of temperament do they have? Are they treated well?

2. Have you ever been to the circus? What were some of the animals you saw? What kinds of things were these animals trained to do? Is it ethical to use animals in circuses for entertainment?

3. Do you think it's good for people to have animals as pets? If so, what kinds of animals make good pets? Have you ever had a pet? What was it? What was its name?

4. Many animals such as the elephant, the giant panda, and the koala bear are endangered species, that is, they are close to extinction. Do you feel human beings have a responsibility to try to save these animals from extinction? Why or why not?

5. Do animals have rights equal to humans? Why or why not?

B. The Listening Expansion

Task 1.   **Completing a Sketch**

I am going to talk about my two sisters, Alice and Betty. Alice and Betty are very different from each other. Look at the pictures of Alice and Betty below. As you can see, these sketches are incomplete. I will describe my sisters in detail and you will complete the sketches from my description. For example, I will say, "My two sisters have different hair styles. Alice has short, curly hair while Betty has long, straight hair." Now take your pencil or pen and draw short, curly hair on Alice and long, straight hair on Betty. Don't worry about how well you draw. Just do your best and have fun completing the sketches.

Alice

Betty

How did you do? Were you able to get all the details? Did you complete the sketches? Listen again as I describe my sisters. This will give you a chance to fill in any details you missed the first time.

After you have listened to the story for the second time, compare your sketches with another student's sketches or with the sketches in the back of the book.

CHECK YOUR ANSWERS ▶

Task 2.

Listening to a Dictation

I'd like to tell you about my two brothers, Charles and David. Look at the pictures. Charles and David are a lot alike. They have many similarities. I am going to tell you some things that are very similar about Charles and David. I want you to write exactly what I say. This is a dictation. Be careful with the spelling and punctuation. Use your pictures to help you. Remember to write exactly what I say. Are you ready?

1. _____

2. _____

3. _____

CHECK YOUR ANSWERS ▶   4. _____

LISTENING FACTOIDS

#1 Listen to a talk about a young elephant who appeared to think he was a buffalo.

#2 An elephant's trunk is a combination of its nose and its upper lip. The trunk of an adult elephant measures 5 feet (1.5 meters) and weighs about 300 pounds (136 kilograms). Listen to the many ways that an elephant uses its trunk.

Lincoln and Kennedy:
Similar Destinies

I. PRELISTENING

A. Listening Preparation

Two of the most famous presidents in American history were Abraham Lincoln and John F. Kennedy. Do you know when each of these men was president of the United States? Do you know what was happening in the country while they were in office? Do you know how each man died?

You will learn the answers to these questions and some other interesting facts about Kennedy and Lincoln. Although they lived in different centuries and were different in many ways, you will learn that there were some interesting similarities in the personal and political lives of these two men.

B. Preview of Vocabulary and Sentences

background the total experience, training, and education of a person; a person's history
- John F. Kennedy and Abraham Lincoln had very different family and educational *backgrounds*.

century a period of 100 years; 1801–1900, for example
- Kennedy lived in the 20th *century*; Lincoln lived in the 19th *century*.

formal schooling education acquired in school
- Lincoln had only one year of *formal schooling*.

coincidences two events that occur at the same time by accident but seem to have some connection; accidentally similar occurrences
- Books have been written about the strange *coincidences* in the lives of Lincoln and Kennedy.

congressman/congresswoman a man or woman who is a member of Congress, the lawmaking branch of the U.S. government
- Both Lincoln and Kennedy began their political careers as U.S. *congressmen*.

U.S. House of Representatives; the House; Congress one of the lawmaking branches of the U.S. government
- Lincoln was elected to the *U.S. House of Representatives* in 1847 while Kennedy was elected to the *House* in 1947. They went to *Congress* just 100 years apart.

civil unrest demonstrations and protests by people against the government
- Both Kennedy and Lincoln were president during years of *civil unrest* in the United States.

civil rights demonstrations marches and meetings to protest unfair treatment of black people and other minorities
- During Kennedy's term in office, civil unrest took the form of *civil rights demonstrations*.

to assassinate to murder an important person in a planned, surprise attack
- Kennedy and Lincoln were both *assassinated* while in office.

the American Civil War the war within the United States between the North and the South from 1861 to 1865
- Lincoln was president during *the American Civil War.*

destiny the course of happenings or events believed to be arranged by a superhuman power or powers, the fate of a person
- There are similarities in the *destinies* of Kennedy and Lincoln.

impact a powerful effect
- Kennedy and Lincoln had a tremendous **impact** on the social and political life in the United States.

C. Rhetorical Listening Cues

In this talk the speaker compares and contrasts John F. Kennedy and Abraham Lincoln. The speaker first talks about the differences between the two men and then discusses their similarities. The speaker uses words and phrases which signal differences, words such as "but," "on the other hand," "while," "whereas," and "different." The speaker also uses words to signal similarities between the two presidents, words such as "both," and "neither," "similarly," "also," and "furthermore."

II. LISTENING

🎧 A. Initial Listening

Now let's listen to a talk about the similarities and differences between Kennedy and Lincoln. It may help you to concentrate on the talk if you close your eyes while listening. Just relax and listen carefully.

🎧 B. Mental Rehearsal and Review of the Talk

Let's listen to the talk once again. This time the talk will be given in message units. Please repeat each unit to yourself silently after you hear it. Remember, don't say the units out loud.

🎧 C. Consolidation

You will hear the talk given once again. As you listen, take notes on what you hear.

III. POSTLISTENING

A. The Comprehension Check

1. Recognizing Information and Checking Accuracy

Answer the questions you hear by writing down short answers in the space provided. It is not necessary to write a complete sentence to answer each question.

1. _____
2. _____
3. _____
4. _____
5. _____
6. _____
7. _____
8. _____
9. _____

CHECK YOUR ANSWERS ▶

10. _____

2. Using and Expanding on the Information in the Talk

a. Recapping the Information from Your Notes. Use your notes to recap the information you learned about the lives and careers of Lincoln and Kennedy. Present the information to the class or to one of your classmates.

b. Expanding on the Information in the Talk. Discuss with a classmate the following questions and issues.

1. Abraham Lincoln provided us with many memorable quotations. Read the quotation listed below and explain (1) what it means to you, and (2) what the quote says about how people do (or should) treat one another:

   As a nation, we began by declaring that "all men are created equal." We now practically read it "All men are created equal, except Negroes." When the Know-Nothings get control, it will read, "all men are created equal, except Negroes, and foreigners, and Catholics." When it comes to this, I should prefer emigrating to some other country where they make no pretense of loving liberty. . . .
   (Abraham Lincoln, 1855)

2. After the death of his son Willie, Lincoln was persuaded by his wife to participate in several séances held in the White House. The president was deeply interested in psychic phenomena and wanted

to communicate with his dead son. Once Lincoln reported that he had attended a séance in which a piano was raised and moved around the room. It was the professional opinion of the mediums who had worked with him that Lincoln was definitely the possessor of extraordinary psychic powers.

Answer the following questions in discussion with a classmate:

(a) Do you believe some people have psychic powers?
(b) Would you attend a séance if you had the opportunity to do so? If yes, why? If no, why not?
(c) Do you believe the dead can make contact with the living?
(d) Do you believe in an afterlife? If not, why not? If so, what is the afterlife going to be like?
(e) Do you believe in reincarnation? Why or why not?

3. There have been many conflicting views of who killed John Kennedy. Do you believe that Lee Harvey Oswald, acting alone, assassinated Kennedy? Explain why you believe in the "lone assassin" theory or the "conspiracy" theory.

4. Which of the following positions would you defend?

Assassination of a head of state is never justified.

Assassination of a head of state may, under certain circumstances, be justified.

5. John Kennedy provided us with many memorable quotations. Read the quotation listed below and explain (1) what it means to you, and (2) what the quote says about homelessness in America or any country.

"If a free society cannot help the many who are poor, it cannot save the few who are rich." (Inaugural address, 1961)

6. What does the following story say about how people "rally around" (or support) their leaders during times of crisis?

According to the polls, Kennedy's highest rating as president came right after the invasion of Cuba at the Bay of Pigs, as the American people rallied to support their president in difficult times, and 82% expressed approval of his handling of the job. No one was more amazed at this development than Kennedy. "My God," he said. . . . "The worse I do the more popular I get."

Former U.S. President George Bush also experienced high levels of popular support after the Gulf War only to be defeated in the election two years later. Is it natural for people to rally around political figures when fighting wars? Should people be careful about doing this?

Task 1.   **A Dictation of Similarities**

The wives of the two presidents were first ladies Jacqueline Kennedy and Mary Todd Lincoln. There were also some similarities between the two women. You will hear five statements about the two women. Listen and write down exactly what you hear about Mrs. Kennedy and Mrs. Lincoln.

1. _____

4. _____

3. _____

4. _____

CHECK YOUR ANSWERS ▶   5. _____

Task 2.   **Detecting Similarities and Differences**

Another interesting similarity between Kennedy and Lincoln was the fact that both presidents had vice presidents named Johnson. Lincoln's vice president was named Andrew Johnson. Kennedy's vice president was named Lyndon Johnson. These two vice presidents shared some similarities and had some differences between them. Listen to five statements about the two men. If the statement tells how the men were similar, circle the word "SIMILARITY." If the statement tells us they were different, circle the word "DIFFERENCE."

1. **SIMILARITY**   DIFFERENCE

2. **SIMILARITY**   DIFFERENCE

3. **SIMILARITY**   DIFFERENCE

4. **SIMILARITY**   DIFFERENCE

CHECK YOUR ANSWERS ▶   5. **SIMILARITY**   DIFFERENCE

LISTENING FACTOIDS

#1 Abraham Lincoln is known as "The Great Emancipator" because he freed the slaves in the United States, but did he really? And does he deserve the title "The Great Emancipator"? Listen.

#2 Most people find coincidences like those between Lincoln and Kennedy fascinating. Do you think these kinds of coincidences have some secret or hidden meaning? Or, do you think coincidences happen simply by chance? Listen to an interesting fact about your chance of meeting someone with your exact birthday at a party.

The *Titanic* and the *Andrea Doria:*
Tragedies at Sea

I. PRELISTENING

A. Listening Preparation

People have been traveling by boat or ship for over 3,000 years. During this time, many people have lost their lives in boating accidents or shipwrecks. Two of the most famous shipwrecks occurred in the 20th century. One wreck occurred in the early 1900s, and one occurred in the mid 1900s.

The names of the ships that went down at sea were the *Titanic* and the *Andrea Doria*. Almost everybody has heard of the *Titanic*. There was a movie made about the sinking of the *Titanic*. Did you see the movie? The shipwreck of the *Andrea Doria* is perhaps not as well known even though this shipwreck occurred only about 50 years ago. At the time of the sinking of the *Andrea Doria*, many news reporters compared the sinking of the *Andrea Doria* with the sinking of the *Titanic*. There *were* some similarities, but there were even more differences between these two tragic shipwrecks. In this talk you will learn about both the similarities and the differences between the sinking of the *Titanic* and the sinking of the *Andrea Doria*.

B. Preview of Vocabulary and Sentences

luxury liner a ship that provides passengers with beautiful, comfortable rooms to sleep in, games to play, and excellent food to eat. It costs a lot of money to travel on such a ship.
- On the morning of April 10, 1912, the *luxury liner* the *Titanic* left England on a voyage to New York.

to shock to surprise greatly; to astonish
- The sinking of these two huge ships *shocked* the world.

tragedy a very sad or terrible event; a mishap; a disaster
- Reports of these two *tragedies* filled the newspapers for days.

heroism great courage and bravery; valor; boldness

villainy corrupt, evil, and cowardly conduct
- As each ship was sinking, there were acts of *heroism* and acts of *villainy*.

coward a person who will not face danger bravely; a person who does not demonstrate courage in the face of fear or danger
- There were some people who acted like *cowards*.

disaster an event that happens suddenly and that causes great damage or suffering; a catastrophe
- There were differences between these great ship *disasters*.

iceberg a large mass of ice that has broken away from a glacier and that is floating in the ocean
- The *Titanic* struck an *iceberg*.

to collide with to crash into; to smash into
- The *Andrea Doria collided with* another ship.

lookout a person on a ship who watches for unexpected danger to the ship, such as an iceberg
- The *lookout* was able to see the iceberg only moments before the ship struck it.

to survive to remain alive after a dangerous situation; to live through a life-threatening event
- Over 700 people *survived* the sinking of the *Titanic*.

to rescue to save from danger or death
- There were about half the number of lifeboats needed to *rescue* all the people aboard the ship.

crew those who operate and run a ship

- The passengers and *crew* of the *Andrea Doria* were very lucky.

C. Rhetorical Listening Cues

In this talk the speaker discusses the similarities and differences between the sinking of two great ocean liners. The similarities are discussed first. The speaker uses words or phrases that indicate similarity, such as "both," "also," and "another similarity." The speaker also shows similarity by giving certain information about the *Titanic* and then by giving similar information about the *Andrea Doria*. For example, the speaker talks about when the *Titanic* left England and what happened to her four days later. And then the speaker tells when the *Andrea Doria* left Italy and what happened to her eight days later.

The speaker also uses certain words and phrases to signal the differences between the two ship accidents. The speaker uses expressions such as "whereas," "another contrast was . . . ," "but," and "however." As with the similarities, the speaker shows differences by giving certain information about one of the ships, and then by immediately giving contrasting information about the other ship. For example, the speaker mentions how many people died on the *Titanic* and then tells how many died on the *Andrea Doria*. The numbers of deaths for the two ships were very different.

II. LISTENING

A. Initial Listening

Now let's listen to a talk about the similarities and differences between the sinking of two great ocean liners, the *Titanic* and the *Andrea Doria*. If you wish, close your eyes while listening. Just relax and listen carefully.

∩ B. Mental Rehearsal and Review of the Talk

All right. Let's listen to the talk once again. This time, the talk will be given in message units. Please repeat each unit to yourself silently after you hear it. Remember, don't say the units out loud.

∩ C. Consolidation

You will hear the talk given once again. As you listen, take notes on what you hear.

III. POSTLISTENING

∩ A. The Comprehension Check

1. Recognizing Information and Checking Accuracy

For questions 1–5 you will hear multiple-choice questions about the information presented in the talk. Listen to each question and decide whether (a), (b), (c), or (d) is the best answer to the question.

_____ 1. (a) Italy
    (b) England
    (c) New York
    (d) none of the above

_____ 2. (a) They were both luxury liners.
    (b) They were both crossing the Atlantic when they sank.
    (c) People believed that both ships were unsinkable.
    (d) all of the above

_____ 3. (a) The _Andrea Doria_ sank, but the _Titanic_ did not.
    (b) The _Andrea Doria_ carried enough lifeboats for the people on the ship, but the _Titanic_ did not.
    (c) The _Titanic_ had radar; however, the _Andrea Doria_ did not.
    (d) The _Andrea Doria_ carried passengers, but the _Titanic_ did not.

_____ 4. an act of _____
    (a) bravery
    (b) heroism
    (c) villainy
    (d) all of the above

_____ 5. (a) More people died on the _Andrea Doria_.
    (b) Fewer people died on the _Andrea Doria_.
    (c) About the same number of people died on both ships.
    (d) none of the above

For questions 6–11, you will hear six statements about ideas. If the speaker mentioned the idea in the talk, put a check in the box "*I heard this idea in the talk*." If, however, the idea was not mentioned in the talk, but you could infer the idea from the information given in the talk, put a check in the box, "*I didn't hear this idea but can infer it from the information given*." Finally, if the idea you hear was not mentioned, and could not be inferred from the talk, check the box "*I did not hear this idea in the talk and cannot infer it from the information given*."

	I heard this idea in the talk	I didn't hear this idea but can infer it from the information given	I did not hear this idea in the talk and cannot infer it from the information given
6.			
7.			
8.			
9.			
10.			
11.			

CHECK YOUR ANSWERS ▶

Now, you create four statements about the talk yourself. Ask a classmate to listen to the statements and to complete the chart below.

	I heard this idea in the talk	I didn't hear this idea but can infer it from the information given	I did not hear this idea in the talk and cannot infer it from the information given
12.			
13.			
14.			
15.			

2. Using and Expanding on the Information in the Talk

a. Recapping the Information from Your Notes.   Use your notes to recap the information you learned about the sinking of the *Titanic* and the *Andrea Doria*. Present the information to the class or to one of your classmates.

b. Expanding on the Information in the Talk.   Discuss the following questions with a classmate:

1. The expression "Women and children first!" means that all women and children should be rescued from danger before any men are saved. Do you agree with this? Why or why not?

2. It is traditional that anyone who finds a shipwreck like the *Titanic* can salvage all the valuables such as gold, silver, and money. However, even though the remains of the *Titanic* have been found, many people feel very strongly that the *Titanic* should be left undisturbed. Do you agree? Why or why not?

3. Do you agree with this statement? During terrible disasters like shipwrecks, fires, and earthquakes, most people think only of saving themselves.

B. The Listening Expansion

Task 1.   **A Dramatization of Senator Smith Questioning a Survivor**

Listen to and read the following story which will help you to understand the conversations which will follow between Senator Smith and Officer Pitman, a crewman and survivor of the *Titanic*.

There were many terrible questions that were asked after the *Titanic* went down at sea. For example, why had the ship been called "unsinkable" when it actually sank within 2½ hours after it struck the iceberg? Why had the captain of the ship ignored warnings about icebergs? Why did the *Titanic* have only enough lifeboats on it for about half the number of people on the ship? Why were about one third of the people who survived the shipwreck members of the crew?

But perhaps the most terrible question of all was this: Why were some of the lifeboats in the water after the *Titanic* sank *half empty?* The lifeboats in the water had enough room for more than 1,100 people, but only about 700 people were saved. Nearly 1,000 people were left freezing in the water after the ship went down. Many lifeboats were only a few hundred yards away from the people in the water, but those in the lifeboats refused to return and try to save any of the people still in the water. One man who had been floating in the freezing water before he was finally able to climb into one of the lifeboats later said this: "The partially filled lifeboats standing by, only a few hundred yards away, never came back. Why on earth they did not come back is a mystery. How could any human being fail to heed those cries?"

Only a few days after the *Titanic* sank, the U.S. Senate began an official American investigation to answer this question and other questions. The Senate investigation was headed by Senator William Smith. One of the many survivors Senator Smith questioned was Third Officer Herbert J. Pitman. Officer Pitman had been in charge of one of the lifeboats. After the *Titanic* sank, Officer Pitman tied his lifeboat to another lifeboat. There was room for 60 more people from the *Titanic* in these two boats. Listen now as Senator Smith questions Officer Pitman. Listen as Officer Pitman tries to explain why he did not return to pick up the people who were floating around in the freezing water and who were crying for help after the *Titanic* disappeared under the water. Senator Smith begins.

Task 2.

Deciding Whether You Agree or Disagree with Stated Opinions

Listen to the following statements about what you just heard between Senator Smith and Officer Pitman. If you agree, circle AGREE. If you disagree, circle DISAGREE.

1. AGREE   DISAGREE

2. AGREE   DISAGREE

3. AGREE   DISAGREE

4. AGREE   DISAGREE

5. AGREE   DISAGREE

6. AGREE   DISAGREE

7. AGREE   DISAGREE

8. AGREE   DISAGREE

9. AGREE   DISAGREE

10. AGREE   DISAGREE

CHECK YOUR ANSWERS ▶   11. AGREE   DISAGREE

Now explain to your instructor or a classmate why you agree or disagree with these opinions. (Replay the tape or consult the tapescript if necessary.)

LISTENING FACTOIDS

#1 Now listen to these results of a recent survey asking American men if they would sacrifice their lives to save others if they were on the sinking *Titanic*.

#2 Ghosts, submarine tourists, and treasure hunters regularly visit the wreck of the *Titanic* since its resting place in the north Atlantic Ocean was discovered in 1986.

Focus On:
Causal Analysis

Causal analysis is a way of analyzing the reasons, or causes, responsible for a certain result. It is often used by speakers or writers in presenting an explanation or argument. The reasons are usually presented in a certain order, either from most to least important or from least to most important.

Dinosaurs:
Why They Disappeared

I. PRELISTENING

A. Listening Preparation

The word "dinosaur" means terrible lizard. About 150 million years ago, dinosaurs roamed the earth. There were many kinds of dinosaurs. Some of the dinosaurs were as small as chickens, while other dinosaurs were as large as houses. Dinosaurs were very successful animals on the earth for millions of years, but there are no dinosaurs on the earth today. Dinosaurs are extinct. They have been extinct for 65 million years. What happened to these animals that had lived so successfully on the earth for millions of years? Why did they become extinct? No one can be absolutely sure, of course. Many theories have been proposed since scientists began to take an interest in the fate of these incredible creatures.

In this talk you will hear about two current theories explaining why the dinosaurs disappeared from the earth. The theories are (1) the climatic change theory; and (2) the asteroid or comet theory. Listen as these two theories are explained to you.

B. Preview of Vocabulary and Sentences

to propose a theory to suggest an explanation for why something happens; an explanation based on observation and reasoning
- Several *theories* have been *proposed* about why the dinosaurs disappeared from the face of the earth.

to become extinct to have disappeared from the face of the earth
- One theory says that climatic changes caused the dinosaurs *to become extinct.*

severe very serious; grave
- The cold weather finally resulted in a *severe* shortage of food for the dinosaurs.

to dwindle to decrease in amount; to lessen
- The dinosaurs disappeared gradually as the earth became colder and as their food supply *dwindled.*

evidence an outward sign of the truth or falsehood of something
- Today there is new *evidence* that the dinosaurs did not disappear gradually, but that they disappeared quickly and suddenly.

asteroid one of the thousands of small planetlike bodies that revolve around the sun
- This theory is known as the *asteroid* theory.

comet a heavenly body made up of ice, frozen gases, and dust particles. It has a bright head and a long tail of light.
- The asteroid theory states that a huge asteroid, or perhaps a *comet,* hit the earth about 65 million years ago.

to block out the sun to prevent the light of the sun from reaching the surface of the earth

- The huge dust cloud covered the whole earth and *blocked out the sun* for months.

rare earth element one of the uncommon substances, such as plutonium, that is composed of atoms that are all chemically alike

- Scientists recently found large amounts of the *rare earth element* called iridium all over the world.

layer of the earth one thickness of the earth

- Iridium was found in *layers of the earth* that are 65 million years old.

to speculate to make a guess based on an observation and some evidence

- Scientists *speculate* that this iridium was brought to earth 65 million years ago when a comet or asteroid hit the earth.

to debate to give reasons for and against; to argue formally for or against

- Today scientists *debate* the two theories: the climatic change theory and the asteroid theory.

lizard a reptile with four legs, a long tail, and a scaly body

- In the future new evidence may be found that supports a totally new theory of why the terrible *lizards* died out.

C. Rhetorical Listening Cues

In this talk the speaker discusses two possible causes of the dinosaurs' disappearance from the earth. The speaker will use some words and phrases which signal causes and/or effects. The speaker will use words and phrases such as "was caused by," "since," "why," "caused," and "resulted in."

II. LISTENING

A. Initial Listening

Now let's listen to a talk about the extinction of the dinosaurs. It may help you to concentrate on the talk if you close your eyes while you listen. Just relax and listen carefully.

B. Mental Rehearsal and Review of the Talk

Let's listen to the talk once again. This time, the talk will be given in message units. Please repeat each unit to yourself silently after you hear it. Remember, don't say the units out loud.

⌂ *C. Consolidation*

You will hear the talk given once again. As you listen to the talk, take notes on what you hear.

III. POSTLISTENING

⌂ *A. The Comprehension Check*

1. Recognizing Information and Checking Accuracy

For questions 1–4 you will hear multiple-choice questions about the information presented in the talk. Listen to each question and decide whether (a), (b), (c), or (d) is the best answer to the question.

_____ 1. Dinosaurs _____.
    (a) were vegetarians
    (b) may disappear from the earth some day
    (c) were successful animals for millions of years
    (d) disappeared from the earth sometime in the past

_____ 2. The dinosaurs died out _____.
    (a) from breathing too much dust
    (b) from eating too much iridium
    (c) because an asteroid or a comet hit them
    (d) because their food supply was destroyed

_____ 3. (a) Dinosaurs disappeared quite suddenly.
    (b) Dinosaurs disappeared gradually and slowly.
    (c) A comet hit the earth 150 million years ago.
    (d) An asteroid or comet hit the earth 65 million years ago.

_____ 4. Both theories state that _____.
    (a) climatic change killed the dinosaurs
    (b) a food shortage caused dinosaurs to become extinct
    (c) an asteroid or a comet hit the earth 65 million years ago
    (d) there is no evidence which could explain why the dinosaurs disappeared

For questions 5–10, you will hear six statements about ideas. If the speaker mentioned the idea in the talk, put a check in the box "*I heard this idea in the talk.*" If, however, the idea was not mentioned in the talk, but you could *infer* the idea from the information given in the talk, put a check in the box, "*I didn't hear this idea but can infer it from the information given.*" Finally, if the idea you hear was not mentioned, and could not be inferred from the talk, check the box "*I did not hear this idea in the talk and cannot infer it from the information given.*"

	I heard this idea in the talk	I didn't hear this idea but can infer it from the information given	I did not hear this idea in the talk and cannot infer it from the information given
5.			
6.			
7.			
8.			
9.			
10.			

CHECK YOUR ANSWERS ▶

Now, you create four statements about the talk yourself. Ask a classmate to listen to the statements and to complete the chart below.

	I heard this idea in the talk	I didn't hear this idea but can infer it from the information given	I did not hear this idea in the talk and cannot infer it from the information given
11.			
12.			
13.			
14.			

2. Using and Expanding on the Information in the Talk

a. Recapping the Information from Your Notes. Use your notes to recap the information you learned about theories related to the extinction of dinosaurs. Present the information to the class or to one of your classmates.

b. Expanding on the Information in the Talk. Discuss with a classmate why you agree (or do not agree) with the following statements:

1. It's important for scientists to keep trying to figure out why dinosaurs disappeared.

2. We shouldn't worry so much about modern animals that are threatened with extinction since it's natural for animals to become extinct.

3. There is no danger today that an asteroid will hit the earth.

4. Human beings might become extinct someday.

B. The Listening Expansion

Task 1. **Recognizing Possible Causes of a Situation**

You will listen to a description of ten situations. After you listen to each situation described, read the four choices (a), (b), (c), and (d) and select the possible cause or causes of each situation.

For example, you will hear this situation described: "John has a broken leg." What are some possible causes of his broken leg? You will read in your book:

_____ (a) John can't drive his car.
_____ (b) John was in a car accident.
_____ (c) John left work early today.
_____ (d) John went skiing last weekend and fell.

John's leg might be broken because: (b) He was in a car accident. (That's possible.) Or (d) He went skiing last weekend and fell. (That's possible, too.) Choices (a) and (c) do not have anything to do with the possible _cause_ of John's problem. Remember, find the possible cause or causes of a situation you hear described. Are you ready to begin?

1. _____ (a) The set is broken.
   _____ (b) The set isn't plugged in.
   _____ (c) The telephone is ringing.
   _____ (d) You forgot to pay your electricity bill.

2. _____ (a) The park is near her house.
   _____ (b) She doesn't feel very well.
   _____ (c) The weather is warm and sunny.
   _____ (d) She has to study for an exam.

3. _____ (a) The weather wasn't clear.
   _____ (b) The spaceship exploded on lift-off.
   _____ (c) One of the astronauts became sick.
   _____ (d) There was a problem with the computer on the spaceship.

4. _____ (a) He was often late to work.
   _____ (b) He found a new job immediately.
   _____ (c) He was sometimes rude to the customers.
   _____ (d) He doesn't have enough money now to pay his bills.

5. _____ (a) He grew up in Paris.
   _____ (b) He liked living in Paris.
   _____ (c) He went to Paris to get a job.
   _____ (d) His parents lived there in the 1940s.

6. _____ (a) The teacher didn't like Mary.

_____ (b) Mary didn't study for the exam.

_____ (c) The examination was too difficult for the class.

_____ (d) Mary didn't understand the directions to the test.

7. _____ (a) Your doctor is out of town.

_____ (b) You have dialed a wrong number.

_____ (c) Nobody is in the doctor's office.

_____ (d) The doctor's phone is out of order.

8. _____ (a) John was unlucky when he gambled.

_____ (b) It's very expensive to fly to Monte Carlo.

_____ (c) John doesn't have enough money to get home.

_____ (d) John doesn't like to lose money when he gambles.

9. _____ (a) John didn't have a good job.

_____ (b) John had married another woman.

_____ (c) John was killed in a traffic accident.

_____ (d) Mary realized that she didn't love John.

10. _____ (a) He is a soccer player.

_____ (b) He is going to play tennis.

_____ (c) He is getting ready to go jogging.

CHECK YOUR ANSWERS ▶ _____ (d) He has just finished playing volleyball.

Task 2.

Predicting the Ending of a Story: Stating the Possible Results

You will listen to five stories. None of the stories has an ending. You will supply the ending. You will tell what happened in your own words. Tell the ending of each story to your teacher or to a classmate. Use your imagination to complete the story.

1. It's a cold and snowy night. (Listen.)

2. It's the last half of a championship soccer game. (Listen.)

3. A man is walking along the river. (Listen.)

4. You and your friend Bob are sitting in the movie theater waiting for the movie to begin. (Listen.)

5. You are waiting in line at the bank to cash a check. (Listen.)

LISTENING FACTOIDS

#1 Listen to a talk about the unbelievable sizes of dinosaurs.

#2 How long could a dinosaur live? Listen and learn what scientists think about how long a dinosaur might have lived. Two other animals are also mentioned in this factoid: the common alligator and the Black Seychelles Tortoise.

The American Civil War:
Why It Happened

I. PRELISTENING

A. Listening Preparation

In most wars two or more countries fight against each other. However, in a civil war the citizens within one country fight against one another. All wars are terrible, but civil wars are especially terrible because brothers and family members sometimes fight against one another. Like most wars, civil wars are usually caused by disagreements over religion, politics, or economics. In other words, they are fought because of (1) different religious beliefs; (2) political differences; or (3) differences between social or economic systems.

In this talk you will learn about the two main causes of the American Civil War. This war resulted from basic social and economic differences between the northern and southern parts of the United States. The two main issues dividing the North and the South of the country were (1) slavery, and (2) the preservation of the United States as one country.

B. Preview of Vocabulary and Sentences

friction a continuous disagreement over ideas or opinions; a clashing between two persons or groups of opposed views
- One of the causes of the war was the *friction* between the North and the South over the issue of slavery.

foundation a base or support which holds something up; understructure
- Slavery was the *foundation* of the entire economy and way of life in the South.

plantation a large southern estate or farm on which crops such as cotton and tobacco were grown, formerly by black slaves
- In the South there were many large cotton *plantations* that used hundreds of black slaves.

attitude a way of thinking, acting, or feeling; a point of view
- The northern *attitude* against slavery made the Southerners angry.

conflict a long fight or struggle; a war; a clash
- There were other causes of the *conflict* between the North and the South.

domination control; supremacy; mastery
- Many Southerners began to fear northern *domination*.

the Union the United States as it existed between 1776 and 1861; the northern side in the Civil War
- Many Southerners believed that the South should leave *the Union*.

to secede to withdraw from a political alliance or organization
- The southern states decided to *secede* from the Union.

the Confederate States of America the group of 11 southern states that seceded from the United States in 1860–1861
- They called the new country *the Confederate States of America.*

to preserve to keep together; to maintain
- The Civil War *preserved* the United States as one country.

C. Rhetorical Listening Cues

In this talk the speaker explains two of the most important causes of the American Civil War. The speaker uses certain words and phrases to signal the *reasons* or *causes* of the conflict, words and phrases such as:

The main reason . . . ,
Because . . . ,
Because of . . . ,
One of the important causes . . . ,
Other causes were . . . ,
Since . . . .

The speaker also uses certain words and phrases to introduce *results* or *effects*, such as:

As a result . . . ,
Consequently . . . ,
. . . so . . . that . . . ,
. . . resulted in . . . ,
. . . caused . . . ,
. . . led to . . . .

II. LISTENING

A. Initial Listening

Now let's listen to a talk about the causes and effects of the American Civil War. It may help you to concentrate on the talk if you close your eyes while you listen. Just relax and listen carefully.

B. Mental Rehearsal and Review of the Talk

Let's listen to the talk once again. This time, the talk will be given in message units. Please repeat each unit to yourself silently after you hear it. Remember, don't say the units out loud.

C. Consolidation

You will hear the talk given once again. This time as you listen, take notes on what you hear.

III. POSTLISTENING

🎧 *A. The Comprehension Check*

1. Recognizing Information and Checking Accuracy

For questions 1–10 you will hear multiple-choice questions about the information presented in the talk. Listen to each question and decide whether (a), (b), (c), or (d) is the best answer to the question.

_____ 1. (a) in 1861
(b) in 1865
(c) for four years
(d) over 100 years

_____ 2. the issue of _____
(a) religion
(b) slavery
(c) history
(d) crime

_____ 3. The South's economy was _____.
(a) based on cotton and tobacco
(b) dependent on slave labor
(c) both *a* and *b*
(d) neither *a* nor *b*

_____ 4. The North _____.
(a) had smaller farms
(b) grew a variety of crops
(c) did not use slave labor
(d) all of the above

_____ 5. The growth of industry in the North _____.
(a) increased the use of slave labor
(b) resulted in increased population and money
(c) increased southern domination of the North
(d) increased the production of cotton and tobacco

_____ 6. (a) The North abolished slavery.
(b) The South was afraid of northern political and economic domination.
(c) The slaves tried to secede and form their own country.
(d) The South did not want to become industrialized like the North.

_____ 7. (a) the Southern States of America
(b) the Slave States of America
(c) the Cotton States of America
(d) the Confederate States of America

_____ 8. The North went to war in order to _____.
   (a) abolish slavery
   (b) keep the United States one country
   (c) get control over the cotton plantations
   (d) force the South to become industrialized

_____ 9. (a) The slaves helped the North.
   (b) The Southerners did not fight very hard.
   (c) The South depended on slaves to fight for them.
   (d) The North had greater industrial power and wealth.

_____ 10. (a) It industrialized the South very quickly.
   (b) The South realized that slavery was evil.
   (c) It abolished slavery in the United States.
   (d) none of the above

You will hear ten statements about the American Civil War. If the statement is true, put a _T_ on the line next to the number of the statement. If the statement you hear is false, put an _F_ on the line. If the truth cannot be determined _from the information given in the talk_, put a ? on the line.

11. _____   12. _____   13. _____   14. _____   15. _____

CHECK YOUR ANSWERS ▶   16. _____   17. _____   18. _____   19. _____   20. _____

2. Using and Expanding on the Information in the Talk

a. Recapping the Information from Your Notes. Use your notes to recap the information you learned about the American Civil War. Present the information to the class or to one of your classmates.

b. Expanding on the Information in the Talk. Discuss with a classmate the following issues concerning the conduct of war:

1. Martin Luther King said, "We must learn to live together as brothers or perish together as fools." When will people learn to live together as brothers and sisters in a community of brotherhood and sisterhood? Will any event in the future make them forget about conducting war against one another? Do you think it is possible for all people to live together as brothers and sisters? Why or why not? If it is not possible, do you agree that we will all perish together? Why or why not?

2. It is said that "Older men declare war, but it is youth who must fight and die." Do you think this is true? If so, is it fair? Explain.

3. In his 1961 Inaugural speech, John Kennedy said, "Let us never negotiate out of fear. But let us never fear to negotiate." What is the most effective way to negotiate peace in the troubled regions of the world? Do you know of any situations in the world where JFK's advice would be useful?

4. Abraham Lincoln once said, "A house divided against itself cannot stand." What does this mean? Does this saying have any application to today's world?

B. The Listening Expansion

Task 1.

A Listening Dictation

Listen as each sentence is spoken one time. Then write the sentence as it is dictated for the second time. After all sentences have been dictated, they will be repeated for a third time. Check that you have written down each and every word you hear. Notice the expressions that signal "cause and effect" relationships, such as (1) *because*, (2) *since*, (3) *as a result of*, (4) *because of*, and (5) *due to the fact that*.

1. _____

2. _____

3. _____

4. _____

CHECK YOUR ANSWERS ▶   5. _____

Task 2.

Guessing Possible Causes of Events

Listen to the following situations and then give some possible causes for the events described in the situations. For example, listen to the following situation:

A man and woman are sitting at a table in a restaurant. They have just finished dinner. Both the man and the woman look worried about something. The man has his wallet out on the table. He is showing it to the woman. He looks upset. What might be the cause of his upset?

1.

There could be many possible reasons for the man to be upset. One of them might be that he forgot to put his money into his wallet when he left the house. Maybe he forgot to cash his paycheck after work and he doesn't have any money as a result. Perhaps the woman asked him for a loan of some money, and he is showing her that he doesn't have much money. What do you think? You may write your answers on a piece of paper or tell one of your classmates or your teacher your ideas.

2.

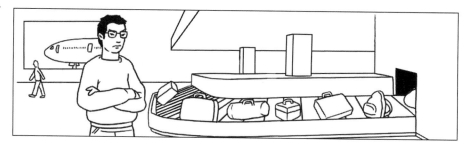

Possible causes: _____

3.

Possible causes: _____

4.

Possible causes: _____

5.

Possible causes: _____

6.

CHECK YOUR ANSWERS ▶ Possible causes: _____

LISTENING FACTOIDS

#1 A book was partially responsible for the start of the great American Civil War. What was it? Listen.

#2 Listen to five interesting—sometimes strange, sometimes sad—facts about the American Civil War.

Endangered Species:
What Are the Causes?

I. PRELISTENING

A. Listening Preparation

Animals like American black bears, Arabian oryxes, Indian tigers, African gorillas, Japanese crested ibises, and Australian giant kangaroo rats, as well as plants like African violets, all have one thing in common. What do these animals and plants have in common? They are all on the Endangered Species List. Being on the Endangered Species List means they are in danger of becoming extinct within the next 20 years. These animals and plants are only a few of the *thousands* of species in danger of extinction. According to the World Wildlife Fund (WWF), by the year 2025 as many as one fifth, or 20%, of the species known to exist today could be gone from the face of the earth.

The loss of animal and plant species is not a new phenomenon. However, in the past, species have generally disappeared because of *natural* causes. For example, some species were not able to adapt, or adjust, to normal climate changes. Other species were not able to compete successfully with other animal or plant species in their habitat. Finally, some became extinct because of some catastrophic event, such as an asteroid hitting earth, as is theorized in the case of the dinosaurs. All of these are natural causes, that is, not caused by human activity.

Today, however, most species in danger of becoming extinct are endangered *not* because of natural causes. Most animals and plants in danger of becoming extinct today are endangered because of *human activity*. There are four major causes related to human activity that are endangering the survival of so many species: (1) destruction and/or degradation of habitat; (2) illegal wildlife trade; (3) over exploitation (excessive hunting, fishing, or gathering); and (4) competition with both domestic animals and with "introduced" (non-native) species.

B. Preview of Vocabulary and Sentences

destruction complete ruin; total damage

degradation worsening in quality; deterioration

habitat area, or environment, where a plant or animal normally lives
- The single most important cause of endangered species today is the *destruction* and/or *degradation of habitat*.

to clear to remove everything that impedes some use
- Forests, grasslands, and deserts, which provide habitat to many plants and animals, *are cleared* to provide residential areas for people to live in and industrial areas for people to work in.

swamps and marshes low wet lands

to drain to draw off liquid gradually
- *Swamps and marshes*, which provide habitat to many animal and plant species, are often *drained* and filled in to provide land for development or agriculture.

to dam to build a barrier across a stream or river to control or raise the level of water
- Rivers are sometimes *dammed* to provide people with electrical power.

oil spills accidental release of oil into bodies of water, usually from a tanker

water pollution contamination of water, often by garbage and sewage

acid rain rain which contains acids that are formed when fossil fuel emissions combine with water in the atmosphere
- *Oil spills*, *water pollution*, and *acid rain* are examples of manmade causes that degrade habitat.

marine animals animals that spend most of their lives in or near the sea, such as whales, seals, walruses, and polar bears

- You probably have seen pictures in newspapers or on TV of dead or dying *marine animals* and birds covered with oil.

illegal wildlife trade the unlawful buying and selling of animals that are protected by the law

- *Illegal wildlife trade* is the next major cause of endangered species.

over exploitation excessive use

- The third major cause that many species are endanged is *over exploitation.*

to compete to strive for or try to obtain the same things as another or others

- Most animal and plant species have to *compete* with other species in their habitat for food, water, and any other resources they may both need.

native animals and plants animals and plants that belong naturally to a certain area or part of the world. For example, kangaroos are native to Australia.

- Unfortunately, this animal (a species of European rabbit) has caused great damage to the habitat of many *native animals and plants* of Australia.

to be running out to be decreasing and close to being gone

- Time is *running out* for many endangered plant and animal species.

C. Rhetorical Listening Cues

In this talk the speaker discusses the four major causes (reasons) why so many plant and animal species are endangered. The speaker uses certain words and phrases to introduce causes, such as "The single most important cause," "the next major cause," "the third major cause," and "the fourth and final reason" as well as "because of," "as a result of," "due to," and "because."

The speaker also uses certain words and phrases to introduce *results* or *effects*, such as "result in," "as a result," "human beings . . . cause," and "has caused."

II. LISTENING

A. Initial Listening

Now let's listen to a talk about the four major causes of endangered species. It may help you to concentrate on the talk if you close your eyes while you listen. Just relax and listen carefully.

B. Mental Rehearsal and Review of the Talk

Let's listen to the talk once again. This time, the talk will be given in message units. Please repeat each unit to yourself silently after you hear it. Remember, don't say the units out loud.

C. Consolidation

You will hear the talk given once again. This time as you listen, take notes on what you hear.

III. POSTLISTENING

A. The Comprehension Check

1. Recognizing Information and Checking Accuracy

For questions 1–6 you will hear multiple-choice questions about the information presented in the talk. Listen to each question and decide whether (a), (b), (c), or (d) is the best answer to the question.

_____ 1. (a) illegal wildlife trade
      (b) over exploitation of plants or animals
      (c) destruction and/or degradation of habitat
      (d) competition with domestic animals and introduced species

_____ 2. (a) tigers
      (b) horses
      (c) elephants
      (d) Brazil nut trees

_____ 3. (a) use of insecticides
      (b) capturing parrots to sell as pets
      (c) over hunting of passenger pigeons
      (d) clearing forests, grasslands, and deserts

_____ 4. (a) use of insecticides
      (b) capturing parrots to sell as pets
      (c) over hunting of passenger pigeons
      (d) clearing forests, grasslands, and deserts

_____ **5.** a _____

           (a) tiger

           (b) sheep

           (c) parrot

           (d) wolf

_____ **6.** (a) goats

           (b) sheep

           (c) horses

           (d) codfish

For questions 7–11, you will hear statements about endangered species. If the statement is true, put a T on the line next to the number of the statement. If the statement you hear is false, put an F on the line.

7. _____   **8.** _____   **9.** _____   **10.** _____   **11.** _____

For questions 12–15, you will hear four statements about ideas. If the speaker mentioned the idea in the talk, put a check in the box "*I heard this idea in the talk.*" If the idea was not mentioned in the talk, but you could infer the idea from the information given in the talk, put a check in the box "*I didn't hear this idea but can infer it from the information given.*" Finally, if the idea you hear was not mentioned, and could not be inferred from the talk, check the box "*I didn't hear this idea in the talk and cannot infer it from the information given.*"

	I heard this idea in the talk	I didn't hear this idea but can infer it from the information given	I did not hear this idea in the talk and cannot infer it from the information given
12.			
13.			
14.			
15.			

CHECK YOUR ANSWERS ▶

2. Using and Expanding on the Information in the Talk

a. Recapping the Information from Your Notes. Use your notes to recap the information you learned about the causes of endangered species.

b. Expanding on the Information in the Talk. Discuss the following questions with a classmate:

1. What animals or plants do you know of that are endangered species in your country or in your part of the world?

2. Is it important to try to save every species of plant or animal? Why or why not? If not, which species in your opinion are the most important to save? Explain why.

3. Are animals more important to save than plants? Why or why not?

4. Can an individual person do anything to help save endangered species? Why or why not? Give specific examples of what can or cannot be done by an individual or a small group of interested people.

B. The Listening Expansion

Task 1.

Listening to Complete a Chart

Complete the following chart about endangered species with information from the lecture you will hear. Follow the instructions in the lecture. At first, just look at the chart as you listen. You will be told when to write information in the blank spaces in the chart. Are you ready?

Endangered Species

Animal	Habitat	Reasons Endangered
Giant Panda	China	habitat destruction; illegal killing for its fur; illegal capture for zoos
Blue whale	_____	over hunted for its blubber, for food, and for whale oil
California condor	Southern California, Arizona	habitat destruction; _____; poisoned to protect domestic animals
Black rhinoceros	south of Sahara in Africa	_____; over hunted for its horn
Snow leopard	_____	over hunted for its fur; killed to protect domestic animals

Plant	Habitat	Reasons Endangered
Floating sorrel	_____	habitat destruction
Green pitcher plant	Southwestern United States	habitat destruction; _____

CHECK YOUR ANSWERS ▶

Task 2. **Listening to Answer Questions Using the Completed Chart**

Now listen to the following questions. Find the information in the completed chart to answer the questions. Write short answers, one word or a few words. Write your answers on the lines below. Are you ready?

1. _____

2. _____

3. _____

4. _____

CHECK YOUR ANSWERS ▶ 5. _____

#1 Is it only plants and animals that are in danger of becoming extinct? Listen to the results of an interesting study that compares endangered languages to endangered species.

#2 If it were possible to weigh all the insects on earth and all the human beings on earth, which would be the greater, the collective weight of all the insects or the collective weight of all the human beings? Listen to find out.

Audioscripts
and
Answer Keys

Unit One/Focus on: Chronology

Chapter 1   Napoleon: From Schoolboy to Emperor

II. LISTENING

A. Initial Listening

Napoleon was a French soldier who became *emperor* of France. He was born in 1769 on the island of Corsica. When he was only ten years old, his father sent him to *military school* in France. Napoleon was not a very good student in most of his classes, but he *excelled* in mathematics and in military science. When he was sixteen years old, he joined the French army. In that year he began the military *career* that brought him *fame*, power, riches, and, finally, defeat. Napoleon became a general in the French army at the young age of 24. Several years later he became emperor of the French Empire.

Napoleon was many things. He was, first of all, a brilliant military leader. His soldiers were ready to die for him. As a result, Napoleon won many, many military *victories*. At one time he *controlled* most of Europe, but many countries, including England, Russia, and Austria fought fiercely against Napoleon. His defeat—his end—came when he decided to attack Russia. In this military campaign against Russia, he *lost* most of his army.

The great French conqueror died alone—*deserted* by his family and his friends—in 1821. He died in 1821, alone and deserted. Napoleon was only 51 years old when he died.

B. Mental Rehearsal and Review of the Talk

Napoleon was a French soldier.
He became emperor of France.
He was born in 1769 in Corsica.
When he was ten, his father sent him to military school.
Napoleon was not a very good student.
He excelled in mathematics and in military science.
When he was 16, he joined the French army.
When he was 16, he began his military career.
His career brought him fame, power, riches, and, finally, defeat.
Napoleon became a general when he was 24.
Several years later he became emperor.
Napoleon was a great military leader.
His soldiers were ready to die for him.
Napoleon won many military victories.
He controlled most of Europe.
Many countries fought against him.
Many countries, including England, Russia, and Austria, fought him.
His defeat came when he attacked Russia.
He lost most of his army.

Napoleon died alone in 1821.
He was deserted by his family and friends.
He was 51 years old when he died.

C. Consolidation

See II. A.

III. POSTLISTENING

A. The Comprehension Check

1. Recognizing Information and Checking Accuracy

1. When was Napoleon born? (a)

2. What kind of student was Napoleon in most of his classes? (d)

3. What did Napoleon's military career bring him? (d)

4. When did Napoleon become emperor of the French Empire? (d)

5. One reason that Napoleon won many military victories was that his soldiers were ready to fight to the death for him. (T)

6. Austria and Russia fought fiercely against Napoleon, but England did not. (F England also fought against him.)

7. Many of Napoleon's family and friends were with him when he died. (F He died alone and deserted by his family and friends.)

8. Napoleon died before he reached the age of 52. (T)

B. The Listening Expansion

Task 1. **Completing a Map**

1. Moscow was the capital city of the Russian Empire during Napoleon's time. Find the Russian Empire on the map. Now write the word "Moscow" next to the star drawn on the Russian Empire. "Moscow" is spelled "M-o-s-c-o-w."

2. Good. Now find the city of Madrid on the map. Madrid was the capital of the Kingdom of Spain. Write the words "Kingdom of Spain" in the correct place on the map. "Kingdom" is spelled "K-i-n-g-d-o-m." "Spain" is spelled "S-p-a-i-n."

3. Another important capital city during Napoleon's age was Vienna. It was the capital of the Austrian Empire. Find Vienna on the map. Write the words "Austrian Empire" in the correct place on the map. That's "A-u-s-t-r-i-a-n" and "E-m-p-i-r-e."

4. North of the city of Vienna was the capital city of Berlin. Do you see Berlin on the map? Berlin was the major city of the Kingdom of

Prussia. Fill in the word "Prussia" in the correct place on the map. Spell Prussia correctly: "P-r-u-s-s-i-a."

5. And last, in Napoleon's time, between the Austrian Empire and the French Empire was the Confederation of the Rhine. Find the Confederation of the Rhine written on the map. Leipzig was its capital city. Write "Leipzig" on the map. Leipzig is spelled "L-e-i-p-z-i-g." Now the map is complete.

Task 2.   **Answering Questions about the Completed Map**

1. Find the Kingdoms of Norway and Denmark on the map. What kingdom is east of Norway and Denmark? (the Kingdom of Sweden)

2. Which kingdom was located south of the Kingdom of Italy in Napoleon's day? (the Kingdom of Naples)

3. There was a small kingdom west of the Kingdom of Spain. What was the name of this small kingdom? (the Kingdom of Portugal)

4. In Napoleon's time, south of the Russian Empire lay the Ottoman Empire. Find the Ottoman Empire on the map. What was the capital city of this empire? Write it down. Be careful to spell it correctly. (Constantinople)

5. Find Finland on the map. Was Finland east or west of the Kingdom of Sweden? Write the word "east" or the word "west" in the correct space. (east)

6. The capital city of England was London. Was London north or south of the capital city of the French Empire? Write the correct word on the blank line. (north)

Listening Factoid #1

The cause of Napoleon's death at the age of 51 on the island of St. Helena is still a mystery. There is no doubt that he was a very sick man at the time of his death. One theory about the cause of his death is that he had stomach cancer. Another theory is that he was deliberately poisoned by a servant. A third theory also suggests that he was poisoned, but not by his servant. This third theory suggests that he was poisoned accidentally by fumes from the wallpaper in the house he lived in. A few years ago, samples of the wallpaper were analyzed and traces of arsenic were found in it. Arsenic is a powerful poison that was used in some of the dyes in wallpaper during the time that Napoleon lived. More than 170 years after his death, people are still speculating about the cause of his death.

Listening Factoid #2

1. Ten people who speak make more noise than 10,000 who are silent.
2. In politics, stupidity is not a handicap.
3. A man will fight harder for his interests than for his rights.
4. Men of genius are meteors intended to burn to light their century.
5. I know, when it is necessary, how to leave the skin of the lion to take the skin of the fox.
6. History is the version of past events that people have decided to agree upon.
7. It is success which makes great men.

Unit One/Focus on: Chronology

Chapter 2   Pompeii: Destroyed, Forgotten, and Found

II. LISTENING

A. Initial Listening

Today many people who live in large metropolitan areas such as Paris and New York leave the city in the summer. They go to the mountains or to the seashore to escape the city noise and heat. Over 2,000 years ago, many rich Romans did the same thing. They left the city of Rome in the summer. Many of these wealthy Romans spent their summers in the city of Pompeii. Pompeii was a beautiful city; it was located on the ocean, on the *Bay of Naples*

In the year 79 C.E., a young Roman boy who later became a very famous Roman historian was visiting his uncle in Pompeii. The boy's name was Pliny the Younger. One day Pliny was looking up at the sky. He saw a frightening *sight*. It was a very large dark cloud. This black cloud rose high into the sky. Rock and *ash* flew through the air. What Pliny saw was the *eruption*—the explosion—of the volcano, Vesuvius. The city of Pompeii was at the foot of Mt. Vesuvius.

When the volcano first erupted, many people were able *to flee* the city and to escape death. In fact, 18,000 people escaped the terrible disaster. Unfortunately, there was not enough time for everyone to escape. More than 2,000 people died. These unlucky people *were buried alive* under the volcanic ash. The eruption lasted for about three days. When the eruption was over, Pompeii was buried under 20 feet of volcanic rock and ash. The city of Pompeii was buried and forgotten for 1,700 years.

In the year 1748 an Italian farmer was *digging* on his farm. As he was digging, he uncovered a part of a wall of the ancient city of Pompeii. Soon *archaeologists* began to excavate—to dig—in the area. As time went by, much of the ancient city of Pompeii was uncovered. Today tourists come from all over the world to see the *ruins* of the famous city of Pompeii.

B. Mental Rehearsal and Review of the Talk

Two thousand years ago, many Romans left Rome in the summer.
Many of these wealthy Romans spent their summer in Pompeii.
Pompeii was located on the Bay of Naples.
In 79 C.E., a young Roman boy was visiting his uncle in Pompeii.
One day Pliny saw a frightening sight.
He saw a very large dark cloud.
This cloud rose high into the sky.
Pliny saw the eruption of Vesuvius.
Pompeii was at the foot of Vesuvius.

Many people were able to flee the city.
Eighteen thousand people escaped death.
More than 2,000 people died.
They were buried alive under the volcanic ash.
The eruption lasted for about three days.
Pompeii was buried under 20 feet of volcanic rock and ash.
Pompeii was forgotten for 1,700 years.
In 1748 an Italian farmer uncovered a part of Pompeii.
Archaeologists began to excavate in the area.
As time went by, much of the ancient city of Pompeii was uncovered.
Today tourists come from all over the world to see the ruins of Pompeii.

C. Consolidation

See II. A.

III. POSTLISTENING

A. The Comprehension Check

1. Recognizing Information and Checking Accuracy

1. At what time of the year did wealthy Romans like to visit Pompeii? (in the summertime)

2. In what year did Pliny pay a visit to his uncle's house in Pompeii? (in 79 C.E.)

3. What did Pliny see when he was looking out over the Bay of Naples one day? (a large dark cloud)

4. Where was Pompeii located in relation to Mt. Vesuvius? (Pompeii was located at the foot of Mt. Vesuvius.)

5. When did an Italian farmer discover a part of an ancient wall of Pompeii? (in 1748)

6. Rome was located at the foot of Mt. Vesuvius. (F Pompeii was located at the foot of Mt. Vesuvius.)

7. Most of the people of Pompeii were able to flee the city and to escape death. (T)

8. Pompeii was buried under two feet of volcanic ash. (F Pompeii was buried under 20 feet of volcanic ash.)

9. Pompeii lay buried and forgotten between 79 C.E. and 1748. (T)

10. The Italian farmer was looking for the ancient city of Pompeii. (F The farmer was digging on his farm.)

11. Tourists come to excavate the city of Pompeii. (F Tourists come to see the ruins of the ancient city of Pompeii.)

B. The Listening Expansion

Task 1.   **Listening for Sequence Identification**

Example 1: John graduated from high school in the spring. He went to college in the fall.

These two sentences are in the correct time sequence. The event in the first sentence happened before the event in the second sentence. Write "yes" next to example 1.

Example 2: He took the final examination on Friday. John studied very hard on Saturday for his final examination.

These sentences are not in the correct time sequence. Write "no" next to example 2.

1. Pliny went to Pompeii. The volcano erupted. (yes)

2. The city was covered with 20 feet of ash. A dark cloud rose high in the sky. (no)

3. A farmer discovered part of a buried wall. Archaeologists began to excavate the ancient city of Pompeii. (yes)

4. A large dark cloud rose high in the sky. People fled from the city. (yes)

5. You learned how many people were killed at Pompeii. You heard the story of the city of Pompeii. (no)

Task 2.   **Listening to Complete and Use a Chart**

The eruption of Mt. Vesuvius was probably the most famous eruption in history. However, the eruption of Mt. Vesuvius did not kill the most people of any volcanic eruption. Let's compare Mt. Vesuvius with some other famous volcanoes. In your book there is a chart with the names of six volcanoes. The chart tells you the name of the volcanic mountain, where it is located, the date of an eruption, and the approximate number of people who died in the eruption. Look at Mt. Vesuvius on the chart. This volcano is located in Italy. It erupted in 79 c.e. Approximately 2,000 people died in the eruption. Now let's fill in the missing information—the information not on the chart—for the other volcanic mountains. Are you ready to write in the information and complete the chart? O.K. Let's begin with the next mountain on the chart—Cotopaxi. It is located in Ecuador. It erupted in 1877, and about 1,000 people died. Write the number 1,000 in the correct place. Now look at Krakatoa. It is located in Indonesia. It erupted in 1883 and killed about 36,000 people. Write the year 1883 in the correct place. Now let's complete the information for Mont Pelée, located in Martinique. It erupted in 1902, killing 38,000 people. Did you write 38,000 in the correct place? O.K. Next fill in the blank for Mount St. Helens in Washington State in the United States. It erupted in 1980 and 60 people were killed. Did you write 60 in the correct space? Finally, let's complete the chart for Mount Tambora in Indonesia. It erupted in 1815, killing 12,000 people. Twelve thousand people died in 1815. Now your chart should be complete.

Famous Volcanoes of the World			
Name	**Location**	**Date of Eruption**	**Approximate Number of People Who Died**
Vesuvius	Italy	79 A.D.	2,000
Cotopaxi	Ecuador	1877	(1,000)
Krakatoa	Indonesia	(1883)	36,000
Mont Pelée	Martinique	1902	(38,000)
Mount St. Helens	Washington State (U.S.A.)	1980	(60)
Mount Tambora	Indonesia	(1815)	(12,000)

1. Mt. Vesuvius (79 C.E.) **4.** Krakatoa (1883)

2. Mount Tambora (1815) **5.** Mont Pelée (1902)

3. Cotopaxi (1877) **6.** Mount St. Helens (1980)

Listening Factoid #1

In 1951, an Australian pilot prevented his plane from being shot down— by flak from a volcano. The plane was flying over a volcano in Papua, New Guinea when the volcano suddenly erupted. It sent ash and flak 36,000 feet into the air. Bits of stone pounded against the plane's wings and fuselage, but the pilot kept control and flew the plane to safety. Incidentally, almost 3,000 people on the ground died as a result of the eruption of this volcano.

Listening Factoid #2

Pliny the Younger saw the eruption of Mount Vesuvius from a distance. On the day of the eruption, the boy's uncle Pliny the Elder was in command of a Roman fleet which was not far off the shore of Pompeii. On seeing the remarkable eruption of Mt. Vesuvius, Pliny the Elder, who was a great naturalist, sailed to shore to take a look at the eruption of the mountain. On his approach to the shore, he was met by a shower of hot cinders which grew thicker and hotter as he advanced. He finally landed on the shore, and went to a house away from the beach. He even went to sleep, but later in the night, the servants woke him up. By then, the house had begun to rock so violently that Pliny and everyone in his household left the house and went toward the beach to escape. Tying pillowcases on their heads, and using torches to light the way, they groped their way to the beach. But it was too late for Pliny the Elder. Apparently, he became tired and lay down on the ground to rest. But when he lay down on the ground, he died. His death was probably due to carbon dioxide poisoning. Since CO_2 is heavier than air, it hugs the ground and makes it impossible to breathe when one is close to the ground. It is likely that others in the area also died of carbon dioxide poisoning if they lay down to rest on the ground below Mt. Vesuvius.

Unit One/Focus on: Chronology

Chapter 3   Lance Armstrong: Survivor and Winner

I. PRELISTENING

A. Initial Listening

Lance Armstrong was born on September 18, 1971 in a suburb of Dallas, Texas, called Plano. Lance began running and swimming *competitively* when he was only 10 years old. By the time he was 13, he was competing in *triathlons* and won the Iron Kids Triathlon. Lance's mother, who raised Lance mostly by herself, recognized and *encouraged* his competitive spirit.

During his senior year in high school, Lance was invited to train with the U.S. Olympic cycling developmental team in Colorado. From that time on, Lance *focused* completely on cycling. By 1991, Lance was the U.S. National *Amateur* Champion. He also won two major national races the same year—even beating some professional cyclists.

Although he was generally doing very well, Lance had his *ups and downs*. In 1992 he was expected to do very well at the Barcelona Olympics, but he finished in 14th place. This was a big disappointment. Lance got over his disappointment and decided to turn professional. In his first professional race, the 1992 Classico San Sebastian, he ended up finishing dead last, 27 minutes behind the winner. Lance's mother continued to encourage Lance through his difficult times.

Things went much better for Lance in the following years. In 1993 he was the youngest person to win the World Race Championships. In the same year, he entered the Tour de France for the first time. He won one stage of the race, but dropped out of the race before finishing it. In 1995, he even won the Classico San Sebastian, the race he had finished last in, in 1992. Lance also won the most important U.S. tournament, the Tour Du Pont, two times, in both 1995 and 1996. By 1996, Lance *was ranked* seventh among cyclists in the world, and he signed a two-year contract with a French racing team. At that time, he was still a few months away from his 25th birthday; everything was looking very good for Lance Armstrong.

However, everything changed dramatically and drastically in October of 1996, shortly after his 25th birthday. At this time, Lance *was diagnosed* with advanced cancer that had already *spread* to his brain and lungs. He almost immediately underwent two cancer surgeries. After these two *surgeries*, he was given a less than 50-50 chance of survival as he began an *aggressive* three-month course of *chemotherapy*. The chemotherapy left Lance very weak, but the treatment worked well. Quite soon after, Lance was declared free of cancer. Lance returned to cycling and training only five months after he was initially diagnosed with cancer. He vowed he would return to competitive cycling better than ever.

However, his French cycling team dropped Lance from the team. They did not believe that Lance would ever be able return to his former level of strength and endurance. Fortunately the U.S. Postal Service Team became his new *sponsor*. With the support of the U.S. Postal Service Team, Lance returned to racing in 1998. After one particularly bad day during one of his races, Lance pulled over and decided he was done with racing. However, after spending time with his really good cycling friends, Lance returned to racing, and again he was off again in pursuit of cycling victories!

Lance's big *comeback* was marked by his victory at the 1999 Tour de France. Lance repeated this feat in the years 2000, 2001, 2002, 2003, and 2004, for a total of six consecutive victories in the Tour de France, the most prestigious and the most grueling of all cycling contests. Lance's Tour de France record may never *be beaten* or even *be matched*. Interestingly, Lance was the youngest person to win the World Cycling Championships in 1993 and the oldest person ever to win the Tour de France in 2004!

In addition to his amazing athletic performance, Lance Armstrong has established the Lance Armstrong Foundation, which is devoted to providing information about cancer and support to cancer victims. He has also written a book about his life and winning the Tour de France, called *Every Second Counts*, and for Lance, every second has *counted*.

Lance Armstrong gives a lot of credit for his success to his mother, whose independent spirit and support for Lance inspired him to overcome all of life's obstacles, both on and off the racetrack. Lance, in turn, has provided inspiration to many, for his courage—both athletic and personal.

B. Mental Rehearsal and Review of the Talk

Lance Armstrong was born on September 18, 1971 in Plano, Texas.
Plano is a suburb of Dallas, Texas.
Lance began running and swimming competitively when he was only 10 years old.
By the time he was 13, he was competing in triathlons.
When he was 13, he won the Iron Kids Triathlon.
Lance's mother raised Lance mostly by herself.
She recognized and encouraged his competitive spirit.
During his senior year in high school, Lance was invited to train in Colorado.
He was invited to train with the U.S. Olympic cycling developmental team.
From that time on, Lance focused completely on cycling.
By 1991, Lance was the U.S. National Amateur Champion.
He also won two major national races the same year.
He even beat some professional cyclists.
Lance was generally doing very well.
But Lance had his ups and downs.
In 1992 he was expected to do very well at the Barcelona Olympics.

He finished in 14th place.

This was a big disappointment.

Lance got over his disappointment.

He decided to turn professional.

His first professional race was the 1992 Classico San Sebastian.

He ended up finishing dead last.

He finished 27 minutes behind the winner.

Lance's mother continued to encourage Lance through his difficult times.

Things went much better for Lance in the following years.

In 1993 he won the World Race Championships.

He was the youngest person to win the World Race Championships.

In the same year, he entered the Tour de France for the first time.

He won one stage of the race.

He dropped out of the race before finishing it.

In 1995, he even won the Classico San Sebastian.

This was the race he had finished last in, in 1992.

Lance also won the most important U.S. tournament, the Tour Du Pont, two times.

He won the Tour Du Point in both 1995 and 1996.

By 1996, Lance was ranked seventh among cyclists in the world.

He signed a two-year contract with a French racing team.

He was still a few months away from his 25th birthday.

Everything was looking very good for Lance Armstrong.

Everything changed dramatically and drastically in October of 1996.

This was shortly after his 25th birthday.

Lance was diagnosed with advanced cancer.

This cancer had already spread to his brain and lungs.

He almost immediately underwent two cancer surgeries.

After these two surgeries, he was given a less than 50-50 chance of survival.

He began an aggressive three-month course of chemotherapy.

The chemotherapy left Lance very weak.

The treatment worked very well.

Quite soon after, Lance was declared free of cancer.

Lance returned to cycling and training.

He returned only five months after he was initially diagnosed with cancer.

He vowed he would return to competitive cycling better than ever.

His French cycling team dropped Lance from the team.

They did not believe that Lance would ever be able to return to his former level of strength and endurance.

The U.S. Postal Service Team became his new sponsor.

Lance returned to racing in 1998.

After one particularly bad day during one of his races, Lance pulled over.

He decided he was done with racing.

After spending time with his really good cycling friends, Lance returned to racing.

He was off again in pursuit of cycling victories!

Lance's big comeback was marked by his victory at the 1999 Tour de France.

Lance repeated this feat in the years 2000, 2001, 2002, 2003, and 2004.

This was a total of six consecutive victories in the Tour de France.

The Tour de France is the most prestigious and the most grueling of all cycling contests.

Lance's Tour de France record may never be beaten or even matched.

Lance was the youngest person to win the World Cycling Championships in 1993.

He was the oldest person ever to win the Tour de France in 2004!

Lance Armstrong has established the Lance Armstrong Foundation.

The Lance Armstrong Foundation is devoted to providing information about cancer and support to cancer victims.

He has also written a book about his life and winning the Tour de France.

His book is called *Every Second Counts*.

For Lance Armstrong, every second has counted.

Lance Armstrong gives a lot of credit for his success to his mother.

Her independent spirit and support for Lance inspired him.

They have inspired him to overcome all of life's obstacles, both on and off the racetrack.

Lance, in turn, has provided inspiration to many, for his courage—both athletic and personal.

C. Consolidation

See II. A.

III. POSTLISTENING

A. The Comprehension Check

1. Recognizing Information and Checking Accuracy

1. How old was Lance when he began running and swimming competitively? (b)

2. Which sports contest did Lance win when he was 13 years old? (b)

3. How old was Lance when he was diagnosed with advanced cancer? (c)

4. What chance for survival was Lance given after he underwent two surgeries? (c)

5. Who was Lance's sponsor when he won the Tour de France in 1999? (d)

6. What is the name of the book that Lance wrote that is mentioned in the lecture? (b)

7. Lance's cancer had already spread to his lungs and brain before it was diagnosed. (T)

8. Lance's French team dropped Lance because they didn't think he would ever return to his former level of strength and endurance. (T)

9. Lance won the Classico San Sebastian two times. (F He lost the first time and won the second time.)

10. Lance is the only cyclist to win the Tour de France five times consecutively. (F Lance is the only person to win the Tour de France *six* times consecutively.)

B. THE LISTENING EXPANSION

Task 1.

History of the Bicycle

The precursor to the bicycle appeared in France in the *1790s*. It was a little wooden horse with a fixed front wheel. Because the wheel was fixed, it could not be turned right or left. This little horse did not have any pedals, and the only way it could be maneuvered was by the rider pushing against the ground with his or her feet.

In *1817*, the German baron Karl von Drais replaced the fixed front wheel with one that could be steered. Now the wooden horse could be directed right or left. The rider still needed to push it with his or her feet on the ground.

The next development occurred in *1839*, when a Scottish blacksmith, Kirkpatrick MacMillan, designed the first bicycle-like machine with pedals and cranks. MacMillan called his machine a "velocipede" and rode it the 40 miles from his home to Glasgow, Scotland in only *5* hours.

In *1866*, Pierre Lallement applied for and received a U.S. patent for a machine that he called the "bisicle." Some people called it a "boneshaker" as it had steel-rimmed wooden wheels. The bicycle got more comfortable in *1869* when rubber tires were introduced. *Around the same time*, the front wheels began to grow larger while the back wheels got smaller, and the first "highwheeler" was introduced in 1872. During the *1880s*, bicycles enjoyed a boom—that is, a sudden growth in popularity. The highwheelers were very popular, especially among young men, as they could go very fast. However, they weren't very safe. Sitting high up towards the front of the bicycle and traveling very fast, the rider could be easily thrown over the front wheel if the bicycle hit a small bump in the road or if a dog ran in front of the bicycle. This type of accident gave rise to the expression "to do a header" as the rider often fell onto his head.

Fortunately, the "safety bicycle" was invented in *1884*. The safety bicycle had equal-sized wheels, a chain, and a sprocket driven rear wheel. The rider was *now* sitting further back on the bicycle and in much less danger of "doing a header." More improvements *quickly* followed. Pneumatic tires—that is, tires with air in them—were invented in <u>1888</u>. Two- and three-speed hub gears came in the 1890s. The last major innovation, the derailleur gear, arrived in <u>1899</u>. No further significant changes were made until the 1970s. In the 1970s bicycles became more aerodynamic. That is, changes in design and use of lightweight but strong materials allowed bicycles to reduce the amount of air resistance they encountered and thus go faster. No doubt there will be further improvements in design and materials in the future.

Task 2.

1. I was born into a royal family and educated by a famous philosopher. I became leader of my country at age 19, when my father was assassinated. I was a great military leader, and at one time I controlled most of the known Western world. I died on June 13, 323 B.C.E. at the age of 32. Who am I? (e)

2. I was born in Skopje, Yugoslavia at the time when it was still part of the Ottoman Empire. I left home early to join a religious community. I spent most of my adult life working to help the poor in India. In 1979, I won the Nobel Prize for Peace. I died in 1997. Who am I? (b)

3. I grew up near the British royal family's estate. I married into the royal family when I was 18 years old and had two sons. I later spent a lot of my time working for charities that tried to help victims of AIDS, domestic abuse, and drug addiction. Millions of people mourned my death in 1997. Who am I? (a)

4. I traveled the Silk Road all the way to China in 1271, where I stayed for 17 years. I was a favorite of the ruler Kublai Khan and I traveled in China and Southeast Asia, including India, as his envoy. Later I returned home to Venice and ended up in prison for two years, where I dictated a book about my life and travels. Who am I? (c)

5. I was born in Morocco at the beginning of the 14th century. I spent 30 years traveling. I visited every Muslim country in the world. When I finished my travels, I wrote a history of my journeys in Arabic, the title of which translates into *Travels* in English. I died around the year 1368. (h)

6. I was born around the year 1167. I succeeded my father as ruler of a Mongol tribe. I was ruthless and many, many people died in battles with my armies. However, I was a great ruler and brilliant military leader. I ruled one of the greatest land empires the world has even known. Who am I? (d)

7. I was born into a royal family. When my father died, I led a revolt against my brother and became leader of my country. I was involved romantically and politically with two famous Romans. After being defeated in battle, I committed suicide so that I could not be captured by my enemy Octavian. Who am I? (g)

8. I was born in 1940. My real name is Edson Arantes do Nascimento, but everyone knows me by my famous nickname. I led my football

team to many championships. I also led the Brazilian national team to the world championships in 1958, 1962, and 1970. Some people say that I was the greatest football player of all time. Who am I? (f)

Listening Factoid #1

Amazingly enough, the bicycle is a more efficient means of transportation than any other method of traveling. It takes much less energy to bicycle one mile than it does to walk one mile. In fact, it can take up to five times as much energy to walk a mile than to bicycle a mile. If we compare the amount of energy a human being uses to bicycle three miles, or about 5 kilometers, we find that this amount of energy would power a car for only about 278 feet, or 85 meters.

Listening Factoid #2

According to Professor Steve Jones, the three most important inventions in the history of mankind were (1) fire, (2) speech, and (3) the bicycle. He says that the invention of fire freed human beings from the power of climate, dangerous animals, and monotonous diets. The invention of speech meant that human beings could begin to build civilization. And the invention of the bicycle—by which he really means modern transportation in general—meant that groups of human beings were no longer isolated, but could travel great distances. Being able to travel much more freely meant that there could never again be more than one species of human beings as there had been in ancient times.

Unit Two/Focus on: Process

Chapter 4   The Internet: How It Works

II. LISTENING

A. Initial Listening

The Internet consists of millions of computers, all *linked together into a gigantic network*. Every computer that is connected to the Internet is part of this network and can communicate with any other connected computer.

In order to communicate with each other, these computers are *equipped with* special communication *software*. To connect to the Internet, the user instructs the computer's communication software to contact the Internet Service Provider, or ISP. An Internet Service Provider, or ISP, is a company that provides Internet service to individuals, organizations, or companies, usually for a *monthly charge*. Local ISPs connect to larger ISPs, which *in turn* connect to even larger ISPs. A *hierarchy* of networks is formed. This hierarchy is something like a pyramid, with lots of small networks at the bottom, and fewer but larger networks moving up the pyramid. But, amazingly, there is no one single controlling network at the top. Instead, there are dozens of high-level networks, which agree to connect with each other. It is through this process that everyone on the Internet is able to connect with everyone else on the Internet, no matter where he or she is in the world.

How does information that leaves one computer travel through all of these networks, and arrive at its destination, another computer, in a fraction of a second?

The process depends on routers. Routers are specialized computers whose job is to direct the information through the networks. The data, or information, in an e-mail message, a Web page, or a file is first *broken down* into tiny packets. Each of these packets has the address of the sender and of the receiver, and information on how to put the packets back together. Each of these packets is then sent off through the Internet. When a packet reaches a router, the router reads its destination address. The router then decides the best *route* to send the packet on its way to its *destination*. All the packets might take the same route or they might all go different routes. Finally, when all the packets reach their destination, they are put back into the correct order.

To help you understand this process, I'm going to ask you to think of these packets of information as electronic postcards. *Imagine* that you want to send a friend a book, but you can send it only as postcards. First, you would have to cut up each of the pages of the book to the size of postcards. Next, you would need to write your address and the address of your friend on each of these postcards. You would also need to number the postcards so that your friend could put them in the correct order after he receives the postcards. After completing these steps, you would put all the postcards in the mail. You would have no way to know how each postcard traveled to reach your friend. Some might go by truck, some by train, some by plane, some by boat. Some might go by all four ways. Along the way, many *postal agents* may look at the addresses on the postcards in order to decide the best route to send them off on to reach their destination. The postcards would probably arrive at different times. But finally, after all of the postcards had arrived, your friend would be able to put them back in the correct order and read the book.

This is the same way that information is sent over the Internet using the network of routers, but of course it happens much, much faster!

B. Mental Rehearsal and Review of the Talk

The Internet consists of millions of computers.
These computers are linked together into a gigantic network.
These computers are equipped with special communication software.
Communication software is used to contact the Internet Service Provider, or ISP.
An ISP is a company.
An ISP provides Internet service for a monthly charge.
Local ISPs connect to larger ISPs.
Larger ISPs connect to even larger ISPs.
A hierarchy of networks is formed.
A hierarchy is like a pyramid.
There are lots of small networks at the bottom of the pyramid.
There are fewer but larger networks at the top of the pyramid.
There is no one single controlling network at the top.
Instead, there are dozens of high-level networks.
These high-level networks agree to connect with each other.
How does information travel through these networks?
How does it arrive at its destination in a fraction of a second?
The process depends on routers.
Routers are specialized computers.
Routers direct the information, or data, through the networks.
The information in an e-mail, Web page, or file is broken down.
The information is broken down into tiny packets.
Each packet has the address of the sender and the address of the receiver.
Each packet has information on how to put the packets back together.
Each packet is sent off through the Internet.
When a packet reaches a router, the router reads its destination address.
The router decides on the best route to send the packet.
All the packets might take the same route.
The packets might all go different routes.
Finally, all the packets reach their destination.
The packets are put back into correct order.

To understand this process, think of these packets of information as electronic postcards.

Imagine that you want to send a friend a book.

You can only send this book as postcards.

You would have to do the following things:

Cut up each of the pages of the book.

Cut the pages to the size of postcards.

Write your address on each postcard.

Write your friend's address on each postcard.

Number the postcards.

Put all the postcards in the mail.

Many postal agents may look at the destinations addresses.

They may send the postcards on the same route.

They may send them on different routes.

Some postcards might go by truck.

Some might go by train.

Some might go by plane and some by boat.

Some might go by all four ways.

The postcards would probably arrive at different times.

Your friend could put the postcards in the correct order and read the book.

This is the same way information is sent over the Internet using the network of routers.

C. Consolidation

See II. A.

III. POSTLISTENING

A. The Comprehension Check

1. Recognizing Information and Checking Accuracy

1. What is the Internet? (d)

2. What is a router? (c)

3. What is carried on every tiny packet of information that travels through the Internet? (d)

4. What is a router compared to in the lecture? (b)

5. The Internet is controlled by one gigantic ISP. (F There is no one controlling network at the top.)

6. Routers can send the packets of information in one e-mail message over many different routes to their destination. (T)

7. The lecturer compares the tiny packets of information that travel through the Internet to electronic post cards. (T)

Task 1.   **Connecting the Process**

Once you decide that you need good antivirus software, (1) *the first thing* to do is to see whether your computer already has an antivirus program pre-installed. You can do this by going to Programs on your Start menu and looking for an antivirus software program. If you find there is an antivirus program already installed, (2) *first* check to see if it is activated. (3) *Then* determine whether it is up to date. (4) *Finally*, consider whether it's the best software for your needs. If, (5) *after completing* this process, you decide you need to purchase antivirus software, here are (6) *some steps* you can follow.

(7) *First*, ask friends and colleagues for their recommendations. (8) *After that*, go to the Internet to read several reviews of antivirus software programs. You will see that there are some free antivirus software programs available to be downloaded. If one of them suits your needs, (9) *then* your search may be over. If not, (10) *after reading* many reviews, select a few software programs to consider purchasing. (11) *The next step* is to test them, if possible. Many programs' Web sites allow you to download them for a trial period. (12) *In the meantime*, compare prices of these programs. (13) *After completing* all these steps, you should be ready to purchase your software. If your computer already has an antivirus software program, be sure to uninstall it (14) *before installing* your new software. (15) *Finally*, install your new antivirus software, following the manufacturer's direction, carefully. Keep in mind that antivirus software must be continuously updated to be effective.

Task 2.   **How to Be a Courteous E-mail Correspondent**

    a. Check your e-mail regularly.
    b. Keep your e-mail messages brief.
    c. Be careful how you express yourself.
    d. Don't forward somebody else's e-mail without permission.
    e. Put a clear subject title in the subject box.

Listening Factoid #1

Jeff Hancock, a scientist at Cornell University, asked 30 students to keep a communication diary for a week. The students wrote down the numbers of conversations they had either face-to-face or on the telephone and the number of e-mail exchanges they had, both regular e-mail and instant messages, that lasted more than 10 minutes. They also wrote down the number of lies they had told in each conversation or e-mail exchange. When Jeff Hancock analyzed the students' communication records, he found that lies made up 14 percent of e-mails, 21 percent of instant messages, 27 percent of face-to-face conversations, and 37 percent of phone calls.

His findings surprised some psychologists, who thought it would be easier to lie in e-mails than in real–time conversations. One explanation is that people are less likely to lie when there will be a record of their lies, such as in an e-mail.

Listening Factoid #2

If you have an e-mail account, you have no doubt been spammed. That is, you have received unsolicited e-mail from someone you don't know, someone who is usually trying to sell you something!

Most people say that they hate spam. For many people, spam mail is a just a nuisance, but for businesses it's very expensive, as their employees waste considerable working time going through and deleting spam. According to Message Labs, a company that provides e-mail security, 76% of the world's e-mail is spam and it costs businesses approximately $12 billion dollars a year. According to a survey by Commtouch Software, another anti-spam company, in the last few months the number of spam attacks increased by 43%. Their report predicts that within two years, 98% of all e-mail will be spam!

Unit Two/Focus on: Process

Chapter 5   Language: How Children Acquire Theirs

II. LISTENING

A. Initial Listening

What I'd like to talk to you about today is the topic of child language development. I know that you all are trying to develop a second language, but for a moment, let's think about a related topic: How children develop their first language. What do we know about how babies develop their language and communication ability? Well, we know babies are able to communicate as soon as they are born—even before they learn to speak their first language. At first, they communicate by crying. This crying lets their parents know when they are hungry, or unhappy, or uncomfortable. However, they soon begin the process of acquiring their language. The first stage of language acquisition begins a few weeks after birth. At this stage, babies start to make *cooing noises* when they are happy. Then, around four months of age they begin to *babble*. Babies all over the world begin to babble around the same age, and they all begin to make the same kinds of babbling noises. By the time they are ten months old, however, the babbling of babies from different language backgrounds sounds different. For example, the babbling of a baby in a Chinese-speaking home sounds different from the babbling of a baby in an English-speaking home. Babies begin a new stage of language development when they begin to speak their first words. At first, they *invent* their own *words* for things. For example, a baby in an English-speaking home may say "baba" for the word "bottle" or "kiki" for "cat." In the next few months, babies will *acquire* a lot of *words*. These words are usually the names of things that are in the baby's environment, words for food or toys, for example. They will begin to use these words to communicate with others. For example, if a baby holds up an empty juice cup and says "juice," to his father, the baby seems to be saying, "I want more juice, Daddy" or "May I have more juice, Daddy?" This word "juice" is really a one-word sentence.

The next stage of language acquisition begins around the age of 18 months, when the babies begin to say two-word sentences. They begin to use a kind of grammar to put these words together. The speech they produce is called *"telegraphic"* speech because the babies omit all but the most *essential* words. An English-speaking child might say something like "Daddy, up" which actually could mean "Daddy, pick me up, please." Then, between two and three years of age, young children begin to learn more and more grammar. For example, they begin to use the past tense of verbs. In other words, they begin to learn the rule for making the past tense of many verbs. The children begin to say things such as "I walked home" and "I kissed Mommy." They also begin to *overgeneralize* this new grammar rule and make a lot of grammar mistakes. For example, children often say such things as "I goed to bed" instead of "I went to bed," or "I eated ice cream" instead of "I ate ice cream." In other words, the children have learned the past tense rule for regular verbs such as "walk" and "kiss," but they haven't learned that they cannot use this rule for all verbs. Some verbs like "eat" are irregular, and the past tense forms for irregular verbs must be learned individually. Anyhow, these mistakes are normal, and the children will soon learn to use the past tense for regular and irregular verbs correctly. The children then continue to learn other grammatical structures in the same way.

If we stop to think about it, actually it's quite amazing how quickly babies and children all over the world learn their language and how similar the process is for babies all over the world.

Do you remember anything about how you learned your first language during the early years of your life? Think about the process for a minute. What was your first word? Was it "mama" or maybe "papa"? Now think also about the process of learning English as a second language. Can you remember the first word you learned in English? I doubt that it was "mama." Now, think about some of the similarities and differences involved in the processes of child and adult language learning. We'll talk about some similarities and differences in the first and second language learning processes tomorrow. See you then.

B. Mental Rehearsal and Review of the Talk

Today I'd like to talk about the topic of child language development.
How do children develop their first language?
What do we know about how babies develop their language and communication ability?
We know babies are able to communicate as soon as they are born.
We know they can communicate even before they learn to speak their first language.
Babies are able to communicate as soon as they are born.
At first, they communicate by crying.
This crying lets their parents know how they feel.
Their parents know if they are hungry, or unhappy, or uncomfortable.
Babies soon begin to acquire language.
The first stage begins a few weeks after birth.
They start to make cooing noises.
Around four months babies begin to babble.
All babies begin to babble at the same age.
They all make the same babbling noises.
By ten months the babbling of babies sounds different.
At this time a new stage of language learning begins.
Now babies begin to make their first words.
They invent their own words.
These words are the babies' own words for things, like "kiki" for cat.
Soon after, the babies begin to learn the names of many things.
These things are in their environment.
They learn the words for toys and food, for example.
They begin to use these words to communicate.

They begin to make one-word sentences.

For example, they hold up their cup and say "juice."

The next stage begins at about 18 months of age.

At 18 months they begin to make two-word sentences.

They use a kind of grammar to put these two words together.

This language is called "telegraphic" speech.

Telegraphic language has only the most essential words.

Between two and three years of age children learn more grammar rules.

For example, they begin to use the past tense rule for regular verbs.

They overgeneralize the past tense rule to irregular verbs.

They make lots of mistakes.

For example, they say "I goed sleep" instead of "I went to sleep."

Their mistakes are natural at this age.

They continue to learn more grammatical structures in the same way.

This process is similar for babies all over the world.

Do you remember how you learned your first language in the early years of your life?

Think about the process for a minute. What was your first word? Was it "mama," or maybe "papa"?

Think also about the process of learning English as a second language. Can you remember the first word you learned? I doubt it was "mama." Now think about some of the similarities and differences involved in the processes of child and adult language development.

We'll talk about some similarities and differences in the first and second language learning process tomorrow. See you then.

C. Consolidation

See II. A.

III. POSTLISTENING

A. The Comprehension Check

1. Recognizing Information and Checking Accuracy

1. At what age do babies begin to communicate? (a)

2. Which of the following is an example of "telegraphic" speech? (b)

3. At what age do children begin to use the past tense? (c)

4. At four months of age the babbling of babies sounds the same all over the world. (T)

5. A baby's first words are usually words that he or she invents. (T)

6. A child uses only vocabulary and no grammar before about two years of age. (F He/she actually uses a kind of grammar in making two-word sentences at about 18 months of age.)

7. Children probably say "I goed" instead of "I went" because they hear their parents say this. (F Children say "I goed" instead of "I

went" because they are overgeneralizing the grammar rule for the regular past tense verbs to the irregular verb "go.")

B. The Listening Expansion

Task 1. **Solving a Word Problem**

You are alone in a room. There are two pieces of string hanging from the ceiling. The strings are six feet long and ten-and-a-half feet apart. The only other things in the room are a chair, some pins, some pieces of paper, and a pair of pliers. You job is to tie the two ends of the string together. You may not pull them loose from the ceiling. How will you tie them together?

Solution: Tie the pliers to the end of one of the strings. Start the string swinging in the direction of the other string. Take hold of the end of the other string. You will be able to move close enough to catch the end of the other string when it swings towards you. (You cannot solve the problem by standing on the chair.)

Task 2. **Explaining Steps in Problem Solving**

Take the piece of paper and draw three circles on it. Label the three circles one, two, and three. Okay, now you should have a piece of paper with three circles: circle number one, circle number two, and circle number three. Now take the three coins of different sizes and put them in the first circle. Put the largest coin on the bottom, the next largest coin on top of the largest coin, and the smallest coin on the top. Okay, now you should have three coins stacked up in the first circle, the largest on the bottom and the smallest one on top. Now here is the problem. You are to move all the coins to the third circle so that the largest coin is still on the bottom and the smallest coin is on the top. Here are the rules: 1. You can move only one coin at a time. 2. Only the top coin can be moved. 3. You cannot put a larger coin on a smaller coin. 4. You may move to any circle. Remember your job is to move all the coins to the third circle so that they are in the same order as they are now in the first circle. Don't forget the rules: Move only one coin at a time, move only the top coin, and don't put a larger coin on a smaller coin. Good luck!

Solution: Call the largest coin C, the middle coin B, and the smallest coin A. Call the first circle 1, the second circle 2, and the third circle 3.

1. Move A to 3.

2. Move B to 2.

3. Move A to 2.

4. Move C to 3.

5. Move A to 1.

6. Move B to 3.

7. Move A to 3.

Listening Factoid #1

Have you ever wondered about what the world's original language was? Or whether children would begin to speak if they never heard language? Well, more than 2,500 years ago, an Egyptian pharaoh asked himself the same questions. He had the idea that children who didn't hear adults speaking any language would begin to speak the world's "original language." So he had two newborn babies of poor parents taken away from them. He gave the babies to a shepherd to take care of. No one was allowed to speak to them. About two years later, the shepherd reported to the pharaoh that the children were making a sound like "bekos." This sound "bekos" sounded like the word for bread in the Phrygian language, so the pharaoh concluded that Phrygian was the original language in the world. There was only one problem with the pharaoh's conclusion. He overlooked the fact that "bekos" sounded very much like the noise that sheep make!

Listening Factoid #2

Do you know that grownups use baby talk? Why? To help babies learn to speak! David Sacks, a linguist, says that, "babies in their first year of life learn to speak—first in baby talk, then with the rudiments of genuine vocabulary—by imitating the speech sounds they hear around them. (Often these sounds are addressed to the baby in an exaggerated, singsong form; for example, "How did you sleeeep?" which apparently helps the child to learn.) But some scholars have theorized that language in the nursery is partly a two-way street and that certain family-related words in English and other tongues were formed originally—perhaps prehistorically—in imitation of baby talk. Such words are easy for babies to pronounce. The parent will say to the baby, "Say *dada*" and so the word "dada" retains a secure place in the language. What are these words that are easy to say? While the words vary from language to language, in English they are some of the *"ba," "da," "ma,"* and *"pa"* words.

The earliest speech sounds out of an infant's mouth, sometimes as early as the second month of life, might typically be pure vowels. The sounds *"ah," "ee,"* and *"oo"* are said to predominate among babies all over the world, with *"ah"* as the earliest and most frequent sound. The infant's next step, usually begun before four months of age, is to float a consonant sound in front of the vowel: *"ma-ma-ma,"* the sound of pure baby talk.

Unit Two/Focus on: Process

Chapter 6   Hydroponic Aquaculture: How One System Works

II. LISTENING

A. Initial Listening

The growing of plants without soil has developed from experiments carried out to determine what *substances* (like soil and water) make plants grow. Growing plants in water (rather than in soil)—in other words, hydroponics—dates back many more years than you might think. Scientists believe that hydroponics or aquaculture is at least as ancient as the pyramids of Egypt. Scientists also know that a primitive form of aquaculture has been used in the region of Kashmir for centuries. In fact, scientists believe hydroponic growing actually *preceded* soil growing. They even believe that using hydroponics as a farming tool started in the ancient city of Babylon with its famous hanging gardens. These hanging gardens were probably one of the first successful attempts to grow plants hydroponically.

However, returning to more modern times, researchers at the University of the Virgin Islands have developed a system of hydroponic aquaculture that is both simple and low cost. The system uses gravity to create recirculating water systems in which fish are raised and vegetables are grown. Let me take a minute to explain the process of how this particular system of hydroponic aquaculture works on the island of St. Croix in the Virgin Islands.

To start with, rainwater is collected in a large 3,000-gallon tank. This tank is located on the highest point of land on the island. The tank is so large that it measures about 12 feet in diameter. Once the tank is filled with rainwater, fish are added to the tank and subsequently raised in a large tank. So, first, the researchers collect rainwater in a large tank; then they add fish; the fish swim around and excrete waste into the water.

The next step in the process happens in this way. The rainwater collected in the large tank slowly runs out of the bottom of the large fish tank and into another tank. This other tank holds the waste from the fish. The water is then filtered. After the water is filtered, it is passed through a "bio-filter" that contains bacteria. These bacteria convert any harmful ammonia produced in the fish waste into nitrates. These nitrates are then used to feed the plants in the next stage of the process.

So, what happens next? After the water has passed through this bio-filter, it enters two 100-foot-long hydroponic tanks. Just above the 100-foot-long tanks of water, plants are suspended on *trays*. In this particular case, the plants suspended on trays are lettuce plants. The plant roots stand in the water. Through the roots, the plants *soak up* or *absorb* the nitrates and other *nutrients* in the water before the water drains out of these 100-foot-long tanks into a large reservoir. The reservoir is located at the lowest point on the island. It is now necessary to get the water from the lowest part of the island back up to the highest point on the island so that the water can circulate through the process again. Now, how do they get the water from the reservoir back up to the highest point on the island? Well, a *pump* is used to cycle the water back to the 3,000-gallon fish tank, and then the hydroponic process starts all over again.

The aquaculture scientists say that this relatively simple system produces about 25,000 heads of lettuce, and one ton of fish in a year from just one 3,000-gallon fish tank. A commercial company would need to have several tanks in order to make the process *profitable*, but researchers at the University of the Virgin Islands have demonstrated exactly how aquaculture can be used to grow plants without using soil. The process could help some countries that are looking to develop new methods to produce food in "soil-less culture." Just to give an example, in the case of tomatoes, dirt farmers raise about 3,500 plants per acre. In hydroponics, the tomato plants can be placed much closer together, and it's possible to cultivate as many as 10,000 plants on an acre of land. In the future, we will probably see more and more agriculture being done as hydroponic aquaculture. And many consumers won't know the difference.

B. Mental Rehearsal and Review of the Talk

Growing plants without soil was developed to learn what substances make plants grow.
Growing plants in water dates back more years than you think.
Hydroponics is as ancient as the pyramids.
Scientists believe hydroponic growing preceded soil growing.
Hydroponics as a farming tool started in the ancient city of Babylon.
The hanging gardens of Babylon used hydroponics to grow plants.
Researchers have developed a system of hydroponic aquaculture.
The system uses gravity.
It creates recirculating water systems.
Fish and vegetables are grown in the water systems.
Rainwater is collected in a large 3,000-gallon tank.
The tank is on the highest point of the island.
The tank is 12 feet in diameter.
Fish are added to the water in this large tank.
The rainwater slowly runs out of the bottom of the fish tank into another tank of water.
This other tank holds the waste from the fish.
The waste is filtered out of the water.
The water then passes through a "bio-filter."
The bio-filter contains bacteria.
These bacteria convert ammonia produced by the fish waste into nitrate.
The nitrate is used for plant food.
The water then enters two 100-foot-long hydroponic tanks.

Lettuce plants are suspended just above the water on trays.
The plants soak up the nitrates and the other nutrients in the water.
The water then drains out of the tanks into a reservoir.
The reservoir is located at the lowest point on the island.
A pump cycles the water back up to the 3,000-gallon fish tank.
The process starts all over again.
The system produces 25,000 heads of lettuce and one ton of fish in a year.
The lettuce and fish are produced from one 3,000-gallon fish tank.
A commercial company would need several tanks to make the process profitable.
A dirt farmer can raise 3,500 tomato plants on an acre.
A hydroponic farmer can raise 10,000 tomato plants on an acre.
The process might help countries looking for new methods of food production.

C. Consolidation

See II. A.

III. POSTLISTENING

A. The Comprehension Check

1. Recognizing Information and Checking Accuracy

1. How old do scientists think aquaculture is? (d)

2. Which country (or region) did the lecturer not mention in his talk? (c)

3. What makes the water pass from one tank to another in the hydroponic system described? (d)

4. What does the bio-filter contain that destroys harmful ammonia in the fish waste? (a)

5. About how many heads of lettuce can be produced in a year with the system described? (d)

6. Growing plants in a soil environment predates the growing of plants in an aquaculture environment. (F Scientists believe hydroponic growing actually preceded soil growing.)

7. The width of the large fish tank described is 12 feet in diameter. (T)

8. The large fish tank is 100 feet long. (F The tanks with the lettuce, not the fish, are 100 feet long.)

9. The lettuce plants use the nitrates from the water as food. (T)

10. Gravity takes the water from the tank with the lettuce plants above it to the tank with the fish in it. (F A pump is needed to cycle the water from the tank with the plants above it to the tank with the fish in it.)

B. The Listening Expansion

Task 1. **Listening to Identify Steps**

1. Sit upright with legs extended in front of you. Your back should be straight and your arms should be at your side. (picture d)

2. Now, take a breath and raise your arms overhead so that your arms are straight up in the air over your head. (picture b or f)

3. Next, breathe out and bend forward with your arms stretched out in front of you. (picture a)

4. Then take hold of your ankles. (picture g)

5. Next, rest your forehead on your knees. (picture c)

6. Count to eight. Now, breath in as you bring your torso back to an upright position with your arms over your head again. (picture f or b)

7. Breath out as you slowly bring your arms back to your sides. (picture e)

Task 2. **Taking Your Pulse**

Step 1: Put the middle three fingers of your right hand, or your left hand if you are lefthanded, on your left wrist just above your thumb.

Step 2: Press down a little until you feel your pulse beat.

Step 3: Look at a watch with a second hand or ask someone to keep time for you. Count the number of beats you feel in 30 seconds and write down the number.

Step 4: Now wait a few seconds and repeat step 1 and step 2.

Step 5: If you count around the same number of beats the second time, write down this number also and add the first and second numbers. This is your pulse rate. If you didn't count around the same number of beats the second time, then you should wait a few minutes and repeat steps 1 through 4 again.

Listening Factoid #1

The jackfruit tree of southern Asia bears the world's largest tree fruits. The fruits can weigh as much as 110 pounds. As many as 250 fruits are produced by a single tree each year. People in India and Sri Lanka eat the fruit fresh or make a syrup out of this large fruit. Would you like to eat the jackfruit?

Listening Factoid #2

Did you know that the Aztecs of Central America did hydroponic gardening long ago? How did they do it? First, they built rafts of rushes and reeds tied together with tough roots. Then they dredged up soil from the shallow bottom of the lake, and piled it on the rafts. Because the soil came from the lake bottom, it was rich in a variety of organic substances and nutrients. On these rafts they planted vegetables, flowers, and even trees. The roots of these plants, pushing down towards a source of water, would grow through the floor of the raft and down into the water. The rafts were joined together to form floating islands as much as 200 feet long. On market days, a farmer on one of these floating islands would pole his raft close to a market place, pick his vegetables or flowers, and sell them to shoppers walking by. The shoppers got really fresh (and hydroponic) fruits and vegetables.

Unit Three/Focus on: Classification/Definition

Chapter 7   A Tidal Wave: What Is It? What Causes It?
            How Can We Predict It?

II. LISTENING

A. Initial Listening

A tidal wave is a very large and very *destructive* wall of water that *rushes* in from the ocean toward the shore. Many scientists call these waves *tsunami*. In Japanese *tsunami* means "storm wave." But do you know that tidal waves are not caused by *storms* and that they are not true tides at all? A true tide is the regular rise and fall of ocean waters, at definite times each day, but a tidal wave comes rushing in suddenly and unexpectedly. A tidal wave is caused by an underwater earthquake. Scientists call the underwater earthquake a seaquake. The word "seaquake" is made up of two words, the word "sea" which means "ocean" and the word "quake." "To quake" means "to shake" or "to tremble." When a seaquake takes place at the bottom of the ocean, the ocean floor shakes and trembles, and sometimes the ocean floor *shifts*. It is this shifting that produces the tidal wave. The tidal wave begins to move across the sea at great speed.

Tidal waves have taken many human lives in the past. Today scientists can *predict* when a tidal wave will hit land. They use a seismograph to do this. A seismograph is an instrument that records the strength, the direction, and the length of time of an earthquake or seaquake. It is not possible to hold back a tidal wave, but it is possible to *warn* people that a tidal wave is coming. This warning can save many lives.

B. Mental Rehearsal and Review of the Talk

A tidal wave is a very large wall of water.
It is a very destructive wall of water.
It rushes in from the ocean toward the shore.
Many scientists call these waves *tsunami*.
Tsunami is a Japanese word.
It means "storm wave."
Tidal waves are not caused by storms.
They are not true tides.
A true tide is the regular rise and fall of ocean water.
A true tide rises and falls at definite times each day.
A tidal wave comes rushing in suddenly and unexpectedly.
It is caused by an underwater earthquake.
An underwater earthquake is called a seaquake.
The word "seaquake" is made up of two words.
The word "sea" means "ocean."
"To quake" means "to shake" or "to tremble."

During a seaquake the ocean floor shakes and trembles.
The ocean floor also sometimes shifts.
The shifting causes the tidal wave.
The tidal wave moves across the sea.
It moves at great speed.
Tidal waves have taken many lives in the past.
Today scientists can predict when a tidal wave will hit land.
They use a seismograph.
A seismograph records the strength and the direction of a seaquake.
It also records the length of time of a seaquake.
It is not possible to hold back a tidal wave.
It is possible to warn people that a tidal wave is coming.
This warning can save many lives.

C. Consolidation

See II. A.

III. POSTLISTENING

A. The Comprehension Check

1. Recognizing Information and Checking Accuracy

2. They can predict when a tidal wave will hit land. (c)

3. It is caused by a seaquake. (d)

4. It is a synonym for "underwater earthquake." (b)

5. During a seaquake, it shakes, trembles, and sometimes shifts. (e)

6. It records the strength, the direction, and the length of time of earthquakes. (f)

B. The Listening Expansion

Task 1.   Filling In Information and Answering Questions

1 Down	It's a word with five letters. It means a heavy fall of rain or snow with much wind.
10 Down	It's a word with seven letters. It's what scientists do when they say a tidal wave will hit land.
15 Across	It's a five-letter word that is plural. These result from the motion of ocean water and are sometimes very large.
25 Across	It's a ten-letter word that begins with the letter "s." They're people who collect and study scientific information.
25 Down	It's a three-letter word. It's a synonym for the word "ocean."

30 Down   It's a four-letter word. It's the regular rise and fall of the ocean at different times each day.

37 Across   It's a four-letter word that begins with the letter "w." It's what scientists do when they tell people that they are in danger.

1 S	2 E	3 I	4 S	5 M	6 O	7 G	8 R	9 A	10 P	11 H
12 T									13 R	
14 O					15 W	16 A	17 V	18 E	19 S	
20 R								21 D		
22 M								23 I		
								24 C		
	25 S	26 C	27 I	28 E	29 N	30 T	31 I	32 S	33 T	34 S
	35 E					36 I				
37 W	38 A	39 R	40 N			41 D				
						42 E				

Task 2.

Catching and Correcting Mistakes in Information

Shortly after noon today, a severe earthquake struck the northwestern coast of Japan. A group of about 50 people, including 43 schoolchildren, were caught in a tidal wave that hit the coast 30 minutes after the earthquake. The children had just left their school bus and were headed toward the beach for a seashore picnic. At that moment a 12-foot-high tidal wave hit the beach. The wave carried the children out to sea. At this time 13 children are reported missing.

It is further reported that the quake also caused fires in an oil refinery and widespread destruction of homes. The prime minister of Japan has declared a state of emergency in the areas hit by the quake and tidal wave. There will be further details on tonight's six o'clock news.

1. Fifteen people were caught in the tidal wave. (Fifty people were caught in the tidal wave.)

2. The tidal wave hit the coast an hour after the earthquake. (The tidal wave hit the coast 30 minutes after the earthquake.)

3. A 20-foot-high wave struck the beach. (A 12-foot-high wave struck the beach.)

4. The quake caused widespread destruction of beaches. (The quake caused widespread destruction of homes.)

5. The president of the United States declared a state of emergency. (The prime minister of Japan declared a state of emergency.)

Listening Factoid #1

The largest wave known was not a *tsunami*. It was caused by a landslide that sent about 100 million tons of rock crashing into a bay in Alaska in 1958. The slide produced a single wave which covered the hills on the opposite side of the bay up to a distance of nearly 1,700 feet inland. Then the wave, which was 200 feet high, raced back out to sea. No one was killed.

Listening Factoid #2

The speed of a tsunami depends on the depth of the water in the ocean. The deeper the water, the faster the tsunami moves. In the Pacific Ocean, for example, a tsunami travels at a speed of up to 600 miles, or 970 kilometers, per hour. As the tsunami comes close to the shore, however, the speed of the tsunami drops to about 100 miles (or 160 kilometers) per hour. That's still speedy—and deadly!

As the tsunami approaches land, its speed drops, but this is when the wave begins to grow in height. Tsunamis may rise to 100 feet or 30 meters in height.

Tsunamis occur in all of the oceans of the world, though they are the most common in the Pacific.

Unit Three/Focus on: Classification/Definition

Chapter 8   Levels of Language Usage: Formal and Informal

II. LISTENING

A. Initial Listening

Today I want to talk about levels of language usage. You probably have noticed that people express similar ideas in different ways, depending on the situation they are in. This is very natural. All languages have two general, broad categories, or levels of usage: a formal level and an informal level. English is no exception. I'm not talking about correct and incorrect English. What I'm talking about are two levels of correct English. The difference in these two levels is the situation in which you use a particular level. Formal language is the kind of language you find in textbooks, *reference books* such as encyclopedias, and in business letters. For example, a letter to a university would be in a formal style. You would also use formal English in compositions and essays that you write in school. People usually use formal English when they give classroom lectures or speeches and at *ceremonies* such as graduations. We also *tend to* use formal language in conversations with persons we don't know well or with people we have a formal relationship with, such as professors, bosses, doctors, friends of our parents', strangers, etc. Informal language is used in conversation with *colleagues*, family, and friends, and when we write personal notes or letters to close friends, as well as in *diaries*, etc.

Formal language is different from informal language in several ways. However, today I'm going to talk only about a couple of ways. First of all, formal language tends to be more polite. Interestingly, it usually takes more words to be polite. For example, I might say to a friend or family member, "Close the door, please," but to a stranger or someone *in authority* I probably would say "Would you mind closing the door?" or "Excuse me, could you please close the door?" Using words like "could" and "would" makes my request sound more polite, but also more formal. I want to be polite but not too formal with my friends and family.

Another difference between formal and informal language is some of the vocabulary. There are some words and phrases that belong in formal language and others that are informal. Let me give you a couple of examples of what I mean. Let's say that I really like soccer. If I'm talking to my friend or colleague I might say "I'm just crazy about soccer!" But if I were talking to my supervisor or a friend of my parents', I would probably say "I really enjoy soccer" or "I like soccer very much." Let's say I'm telling someone some news I heard about the police arresting a criminal. To my friend I might say, "The cops bagged the crook." To my parents' friend I might say "The police arrested the thief."

Although the line between formal and informal language is not always clear and although people are probably less formal today than in the past, it is useful to be aware that these two levels, or categories, do exist. The best way for a nonnative speaker of English to learn the difference is to observe the different ways English speakers speak or write in different situations. Television newscasters, your college professors in class, your doctors in their offices, etc., will usually speak rather formally. However, your classmates, *teammates*, family members, and friends will generally speak in an informal fashion. The difference can be learned over time by observing and *interacting* with native speakers.

B. Mental Rehearsal and Review of the Talk

All languages have two general levels of usage.
These two levels are formal and informal.
Both levels are correct.
They are used in different situations.
Formal English is used in textbooks and reference books.
It is also used in business letters, compositions, and essays.
People use formal English in lectures and speeches at ceremonies.
We tend to use formal English with people we don't know well.
We use it with people we have formal relationships with.
We usually have formal relationships with professors, bosses, doctors, friends of our parents', and strangers.
Informal English is used with colleagues, family, and friends.
Informal English is used in diaries, personal notes, and letters to friends.
Formal language is different from informal language.
It is different in several ways.
First, formal language is more polite.
It usually takes more words to be polite.
Words like "could" and "would" sound more polite.
Some of the words and phrases in formal and informal English are different.
The phrase "crazy about" is informal English for "like very much."
The word "cop" is informal English for "police officer."
The line between formal and informal language is not completely clear.
The best way for nonnative speakers of English to learn the differences is to observe.
Observe the way different people use English in different situations.
Television newscasters, college professors, and doctors usually speak formally.
Classmates, teammates, family members, and friends usually speak informally.
Learn the difference by observing and interacting with native speakers.

C. Consolidation

See II. A.

A. The Comprehension Check

1. Recognizing Information and Checking Accuracy

1. Which of the following are usually written in formal English? (b)

2. Which of the following people do we usually speak to in informal language? (d)

3. Which of the following is the most formal way to make a request? (d)

4. Which of the following should not be in a composition you write in school? (b)

5. It's unusual to find both a formal and informal level of usage in a language. (F All languages have two general, broad categories, or levels of usage: formal and informal.)

6. People usually use formal language when they first meet someone. (T)

7. The sentence "Mary is crazy about that music" would be acceptable in a conversation between classmates. (T)

8. The best way to learn the difference between formal and informal English is to look up every new word in the dictionary. (F The best way is to pay attention to how native speakers use language in different situations and to interact with them.)

B. The Listening Expansion

Task 1.   **Labeling the Parts of an Ancient Calculator**

An abacus is a simple manual computing device. In other words, it is a simple manual calculator. An abacus can add, subtract, multiply, and divide numbers. The abacus is thousands of years old. The first abacuses were boards covered with sand or dust in which marks could be made. Although an abacus is very simple, it is a powerful and fast calculator which is still widely used in many parts of the world. Let's label the parts of an abacus. Write the labels for the parts of the abacus on the lines on the lower left side of the abacus. Don't write on the lines at the top of the abacus. We'll use those lines later. Let's begin. The outside part of the abacus is called the frame. It has four sides and is usually made of wood. Write the word frame in the space provided. "Frame" is spelled f-r-a-m-e. I'll spell that again, f-r-a-m-e. The next part you should label is called the crossbar. The crossbar goes from one side of the abacus to the other, that is, from the left side to the right side. The crossbar divides the abacus into two parts, the upper part and the lower part. Label the crossbar. "Crossbar" is spelled c-r-o-s-s-b-a-r. That was c-r-o-s-s-b-a-r. An abacus also has a series of rods that go from the top of the frame to the bottom of the frame. Label the rods in the

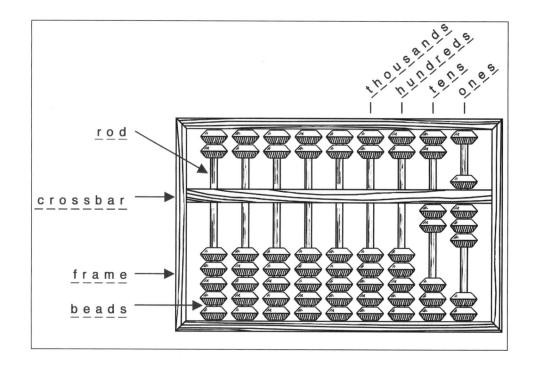

place provided. The word "rod" is spelled r-o-d, r-o-d. The last part you need to label is the beads. The beads are the round balls on the rods. There are two beads above the crossbar and five beads below. Label the beads. The word "beads" is spelled b-e-a-d-s. Okay, now you have finished labeling the four parts of the abacus. Let's go on.

Each rod has a place value. Let's label the place values for the first four rods. Write these labels on the lines on the top of the abacus. The rod farthest to the right is the "ones" position. Write the word "ones" on the line for the rod that is the farthest to the right. Spell it o-n-e-s. The next rod represents the "tens." Write the word "tens" above this rod, t-e-n-s. The next rod represents the "hundreds." Write the word "hundreds," h-u-n-d-r-e-d-s. The last rod we are going to label today is the "thousands." The word "thousands" is spelled t-h-o-u-s-a-n-d-s. Check your spelling of the words "hundreds" and "thousands," h-u-n-d-r-e-d-s and t-h-o-u-s-a-n-d-s. Now you have finished labeling. Continue to listen to learn a little more about the abacus.

The beads represent numbers. For the "ones" rod, each bead below the crossbar is worth one and each bead above the crossbar is worth five. For the "tens" rod, each bead below the crossbar is worth ten and each bead above the crossbar is worth 50. Now answer this question: How much is each bead below the crossbar on the hundreds-rod worth? (pause) How much is each bead on the hundreds-rod above the crossbar worth? (pause) if you said 100 and 500, you were correct.

Let's see how we would add the numbers 16 and 7. First, we would show the number 16 by moving a one-bead, five-bead, and a ten-bead towards the center. Next, we would add 7 by moving two one-beads and five-bead towards the center. Finally, we would change the two five-beads to one ten-bead and then we would have the number 23.

Task 2.

Labeling the Parts of a Modern Calculator

Let's begin in the upper righthand corner of the calculator and continue clockwise. That means we will move in the same direction that the hands of a clock move. Are you ready? The first part we will label is the casing. The casing is similar to the frame. Write the word "casing," c-a-s-i-n-g. The next nine parts we will label are different kinds of keys. The word "key" is already labeled to save time. The first key is the clear key: "clear," c-l-e-a-r. The next key is the clear entry key, clear entry key. "Entry" is spelled e-n-t-r-y. The next key is the square root key, square root key. "Square" is spelled s-q-u-a-r-e. "Root" is spelled r-o-o-t. Let's continue moving in a clockwise direction. The next key is called the equals key. "Equals" is spelled e-q-u-a-l-s. The next keys we are going to label are the arithmetic function keys, the arithmetic function keys. "Arithmetic" is spelled a-r-i-t-h-m-e-t-i-c. "Function" is spelled f-u-n-c-t-i-o-n. Let me repeat those: a-r-i-t-h-m-e-t-i-c and f-u-n-c-t-i-o-n. The next key is the percent key, p-e-r-c-e-n-t. Now label the decimal key. "Decimal" is spelled d-e-c-i-m-a-l. Now we are ready to label the number entry keys, the number entry keys. You already have the word "entry" you can copy. The word "number" is spelled n-u-m-b-e-r. We're almost finished. We have only three more parts to label. The next keys are the memory function keys. "Memory" is spelled m-e-m-o-r-y. You already have the word "function" you can copy. Now label the display. "Display" is spelled d-i-s-p-l-a-y. Finally, we come to the on/off switch. Write the word "on" to the left of the slash and the word "off" to the right of the slash. "Switch" is spelled s-w-i-t-c-h.

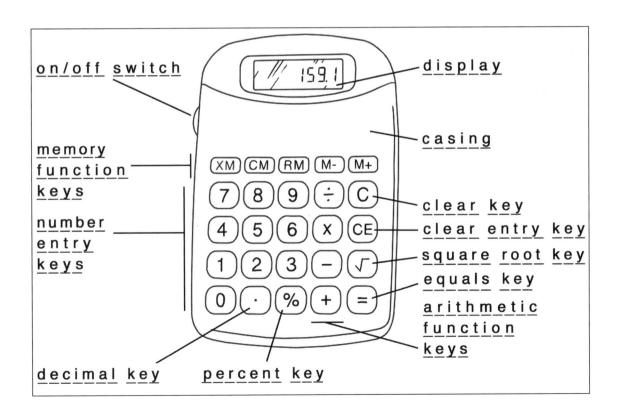

Listening Factoid #1

The *Oxford English Dictionary*, often referred to as the *OED*, contained 414,825 words when it was finally completed in 1928. The *OED* had been started 71 years earlier. Yes, it took 71 years to complete this dictionary. However, this was not the longest time it ever took to complete a dictionary. One dictionary of the German language took 106 years. Another dictionary of the Italian language was begun in 1863 and still isn't finished.

Listening Factoid #2

The slang words *swell*, *groovy*, and *cool* all have about the same meaning. *Swell*, *groovy*, and *cool* all mean something good—something desirable. The difference between these words is mostly generational. That is, people growing up in the 1930s, '40s, and '50s often used the word *swell* when they really liked something. The word *groovy*, which means about the same thing, became popular in the 1960s. In the 1970s, the slang word *cool* became popular. The word *cool* is still used today, but *swell* and *groovy* are not used very much at all, especially not by anyone born in the 1970s or later.

Unit Three/Focus on: Classification/Definition

Chapter 9   Power: The Kinds People Use and Abuse

II. LISTENING

A. Initial Listening

John Mack, who is the author of a book about power, says that the need for a sense of personal power is one of the primary forces in human life. On the other hand, he also says that a feeling of powerlessness is one of the most *disturbing* of human *emotions*—a feeling to be avoided at all costs. Just what is power?

Psychologists define power as the ability to determine or to change the actions or *behavior* of other people. Psychologists are trying to identify different kinds of power so that they can better understand how people use these different kinds of power to gain control over other people. They are trying to understand how people *manipulate other people for* good and *evil purposes.* Psychologists have identified five basic types of power, and I'd like to talk about each of these types briefly in the next few minutes.

The first type of power is called **information** power. Some psychologist believe that information power is one of the most effective types of power and control. The person who has information that other people want and need, but do not have, *is in a position of power.* Why is this? Well, most people like to receive and have information. Having information increasing a person's *own sense of power.* People who provide information can manipulate those who do not have information. Often, when people receive information, they don't know that they are being manipulated by those who provided the information. The psychologist named Edwards says, for example, that newspapers provide a lot of information to their readers, and that these newspaper readers generally believe the information they read. Many readers do not question the *accuracy* of the reports about world events they read in the newspapers.

A second type of power is called **referent** power. For example, a person may want to behave like the members of a particular group, such as a soccer team (or a group of classmates), or a person may identify with and want to be like a certain teacher, a friend, or, say, a rock star. If you *identify with another person*, that person has power over you, and that person can influence your actions and behavior. Many people *imitate* and are controlled by the people they identify with. Let me give you a sad example of the use of this type of power for evil purposes. In the 1970s in Jonestown, Guyana, more than 900 people *committed suicide* when their religious leader Jim Jones told them to kill themselves. They did what he told them to do because he had referent power over them. They identified with him; they believed him, and they did what he told them to do. More recently a man named David

Koresh controlled the lives and destinies of a small community of men, women, and children in *Waco, Texas.* Most of the people in his community died in a fire, along with their leader, during a confrontation with U.S. government agents.

A third kind of power is classified as **legitimate** power. Government officials, according to Edwards, have a lot of legitimate power. When the government decides to raise taxes or make people go to war, most people will do what their government officials tell them to do. One psychologist reported on an experiment that showed an example of this type of power. In this experiment, a researcher asked people on the street to move away from a bus stop. When he was dressed as *a civilian*, few people moved away from the bus stop. When the researcher was dressed as *a guard*, most people moved away from the bus stop. The guard's uniform seemed to give the researcher a look of legitimate power.

A fourth kind of power is called **expert** power. An expert is a person who is very skilled in some area, such as sports, or who knows a lot about something, such as computers. Most people *are impressed* by the skills or knowledge of an expert. Some of these "experts" use their skills at playing sports or knowing about computers to gain power and influence—and to gain money or admiration, according to Edwards. In other words, they use their expertise to gain power.

Finally, **reward** or **coercive** power is used by people who have the power to reward or to punish another person's actions or behavior. Giving a reward will change people's behavior because it offers people *a chance for gain.* Giving a punishment may or may not cause people to do what the powerful person wants them to do, but the changes may not last for a long time. The person who uses coercive power may also have to carefully watch that the less powerful person does, in fact, change his or her actions or behavior.

To sum up, then, power may be gained in many ways. It may come from having information that other people want or need; it may come from being a referent for other people to identify with or to imitate; it may come from having an official, or legitimate, position of authority; it may come from having skills or expertise; or it may come from having the power to reward or punish people. We all exercise one or more of these various kinds of power over other people, and other people will try to exercise one or more of these kinds of power over us throughout our lives.

The need for a sense of personal power is one of the primary forces in human life.

A feeling of powerlessness is one of the most disturbing of human emotions.

A feeling of powerlessness is to be avoided at all costs.

Just what is power?

Power is the ability to determine or change the actions of other people.

Psychologists want to understand how people use power to control other people.

People use power to manipulate others for good or evil purposes.

There are five basic types of power:

Information power is one of the most effective types of power.

The person who has information that other people want and need is in a position of power.

Having information increases a person's sense of power.

People often don't know they are being manipulated by those who provide information.

Many newspaper readers don't question the accuracy of the world reports they read.

If you identify with another person, that person has power over you.

That person can influence your actions and behavior.

Many people imitate and are controlled by people they identify with.

In Jonestown, Guyana, 900 people committed suicide.

They did this because their leader told them to kill themselves.

Their leader had referent power over them.

In Texas, Koresh controlled the lives and destinies of a community of men, women, and children.

Government officials have legitimate power.

Most people will do what their government officials tell them to do.

An experiment showed an example of legitimate power.

A researcher dressed as a civilian asked people to move away from a bus stop.

The people did not move away.

A researcher dressed as a guard asked them to move away from the bus stop.

When the "guard" asked them to move away, most people moved away.

The guard's uniform gave the researcher a look of legitimate power.

An expert is a person who is skilled in some area, such as sports.

An expert is a person who knows a lot about something, such as computers.

Some experts use their skills to gain power, influence, money, and admiration.

Reward or coercive power is used to reward or punish people's actions or behavior.

A reward offers people a chance for gain.

Giving a punishment may or may not cause people to do what the powerful person wants.

The change in behavior may not last for long when a punishment is given.

Power may be gained in many ways.

Power may come from having information people want or need.

Power may come from being a referent for other people.

Power may come from having position of authority.

Power may come from having skill or expertise.

Power may come from having the power to reward or punish.

We all exercise one or more of these kinds of power over people.

Other people try to exercise one or more of these kinds of power over us.

C. Consolidation

See II. A.

III. POSTLISTENING

A. The Comprehension Check

1. Recognizing Information and Checking Accuracy

1. What kind of power do newspapers provide to those who read them? (d)

2. If a teenager wishes to act like a favorite rock singer, which type of power does that singer have over the teenager? (b)

3. Which kind of power may or may not lead to changes that the person in power wants and requires? (a)

4. When a government decides to raise taxes on a product like gas, what kind of power is being wielded? (c)

5. Some psychologists believe that information power is one of the most effective types of power. (I heard it.)

6. If a young person wants to act like an older sister, the older sister is a referent of identification. (I can infer it.)

7. Jim Jones used power for evil purposes. (I can infer it.)

8. David Koresh and his followers died in a fire. (I heard it.)

9. Napoleon identified with his father, who used power well. (I did not hear it and cannot infer it.)

10. Government officials have a lot of legitimate power. (I heard it.)

11–14. Students prepare their own statements about the content of the talk and ask classmates to listen to their statements and to check the appropriate boxes.

Task 1. **Naming the Animal and Naming the Category**

1. This animal can be black, brown, white, gray, or one of many other colors. It's an animal that eats hay. It has a long tail. It was often used for transportation. It's a four-legged animal. What is it? What is it classed as?

   The answer is horse. Write "horse" on the blank in number 1. Underline "vertebrate." Let's go on.

2. It's an animal that lives in the ocean. It is eaten in some parts of the world. It squirts black ink to protect itself from danger. It has eight legs. What is it? What is it categorized as? (octopus/invertebrate)

3. This animal does not live in the ocean. It has wings, and it has antennae on the top of his head. It lives only a short time during the spring and summer. It is a very beautiful and colorful insect. What is it? What is it designated as? (butterfly/invertebrate)

4. This animal lives in the ocean. The animal lives inside a shell. Sometimes a lucky person finds a beautiful pearl inside the animal's shell. It is often served in seafood restaurants. What is it? What is it typed? (oyster/invertebrate)

5. It is a tiny animal. It spins a web. In its web it catches flies and other small insects. Some of these tiny creatures are poisonous. It is an eight-legged creature. What is it? What is it categorized as? (spider/invertebrate)

6. It's a cold-blooded animal. In other words, it needs to warm its body in the sun in cold weather. Some are poisonous. Their bite can kill a person. It has no feet; so it *slithers* along the ground on its stomach. What is it? What is it classed? (snake/vertebrate)

7. It's an animal that is born in the water, but when it's grown, it can breathe air. It hops along the ground. It does not have a tail. Some people like to eat the legs of this small animal. What is it? What is it categorized as? (frog/vertebrate)

Task 2. **The Five Categories of Vertebrates: Placing the Animal in the Category**

1. A *mammal* is a warm-blooded vertebrate that feeds its young with milk from the mother's body.

2. A *bird* is a warm-blooded vertebrate that has feathers and two feet. Instead of arms, a bird has wings.

3. A *fish* is a cold-blooded vertebrate that lives its entire life in water. It has fins instead of arms or feet. It gets oxygen from the water, not the air.

4. A *reptile* is a cold-blooded vertebrate that crawls or moves on its stomach or on small short legs. Reptile babies hatch from eggs with shells.

5. An *amphibian* is a cold-blooded vertebrate that starts its life in water. Later, an amphibian develops lungs to breathe air. Then it can live on land.

Animal	Category
1. parrot	bird
2. elephant	mammal
3. snake	reptile
4. alligator	reptile
5. shark	fish
6. salamander	amphibian
7. owl	bird
8. tuna	fish
9. human being	mammal
10. frog	amphibian

Listening Factoid #1

A powerful king named Mithradites lived in Asia Minor almost 2,000 years ago. He was so afraid that someone would try to poison him that, in order to build up an immunity to poison, he spent many years drinking small amounts of poison. King Mithradites was very successful in building up his immunity to poison. No one was able to poison him. However, his immunity to poison proved to be a problem when he decided to commit suicide in order to avoid being captured by the Roman army. To avoid being captured by the Romans, he tried to commit suicide by drinking poison. Unfortunately, the poison would not work. In the end, one of his slaves killed him with a sword so he could avoid capture. The man of great power was put to death by the man who had no power.

Listening Factoid #2

When girls study ancient civilizations, they often learn about societies where leadership roles and decision making were in the hands of the men of the society. Only on very few occasions are they able to identify with those in authority or those who have played an influential role in the society. The ancient kingdom of Kush was unusual in that powerful queens ruled the kingdom, which occupied the area located in the southern part of modern Egypt and the northern part of today's Sudan. The study of the Kingdom of Kush tells the story of a society where women took on roles of leadership—a society where women were highly respected and held positions of power alongside men. Furthermore, during part of its history, it was a queen of Kush that led the Kushite revolt against the injustice of Roman rule and Rome's imposition of taxes on the Kushite people.

Unit Four/Focus on: Comparison/Contrast

Chapter 10   Asian and African Elephants: Similarities and Differences

II. LISTENING

A. Initial Listening

The African and the Asian elephants are the largest land animals in the world. They are really *enormous* animals. The African and the Asian elephants are alike, or similar, in many ways, but there are differences between the two types of elephants, too.

What are some of the similarities between the African and the Asian elephant? Well, for one thing, both animals have long noses, called *trunks*. An elephant sometimes uses its trunk like a third hand. Both kinds of elephants use their trunks to pick up very small objects and very large, heavy objects. They can even pick up trees with their trunks. For another thing, both the African and the Asian elephants have very large ears, although the African elephant's ears are considerably larger.

In addition, both animals are intelligent. They can be *trained* to do heavy work. They can also be trained to do *tricks* to entertain people. In other words, they both work for people, and they entertain people also.

As I said before, the African and the Asian elephants are alike in many ways, but they are also quite different, too. Let me explain what I mean. The African elephant is larger and heavier than the Asian elephant. The African male elephant weighs between 12,000 and 14,000 pounds. In contrast, the average Asian male elephant weighs between 7,000 and 12,000 pounds.

Another major difference between the two kinds of elephants is the size of the ears. Asian elephants have smaller ears than the African elephants do. The teeth are different, too. The African elephant has two very large teeth. These teeth are called tusks. The Asian elephant sometimes does not have any tusks at all. The elephants differ in color, too. The African elephant is dark gray in color while the Asian elephant is light gray. Occasionally an Asian elephant is even white in color! The last big difference between the two elephants is their *temperament*. The Asian elephant is tamer than the African elephant. In other words, the African elephant is much wilder than the Asian elephant. As a result, it is more difficult to train the African elephant to perform tricks to entertain people. That's why the elephants you see in the circus are probably Asian elephants . . . not African elephants.

Yes, there certainly are differences between the African and the Asian elephants, but there is one big similarity between the two animals: they are both fascinating and enormous animals.

B. Mental Rehearsal and Review of the Talk

The African and the Asian elephants are the largest land animals.
The two elephants are alike in many ways.
There are differences between the elephants, too.
What are the similarities?
Both animals have long noses, called trunks.
An elephant sometimes uses its trunk like a third hand.
Both the African and the Asian elephants have very large ears.
Both animals can be trained to work for man.
Both can be trained to do tricks.
What are the differences?
The African elephant is larger and heavier than the Asian elephant.
The African male elephant weighs between 12,000 and 14,000 pounds.
The average Asian male elephant weighs between 7,000 and 12,000 pounds.
Asian elephants have smaller ears than African elephants.
The African elephant has two very large teeth.
These teeth are called tusks.
The Asian elephant sometimes does not have any tusks.
The African elephant is dark gray in color.
The Asian elephant is light gray.
Occasionally an Asian elephant is even white.
The Asian elephant is tamer than the African elephant.
The African elephant is much wilder than the Asian elephant.
The elephants you see in the circus are probably Asian elephants.

C. Consolidation

See II. A.

III. POSTLISTENING

A. The Comprehension Check

1. Recognizing Information and Checking Accuracy

1. What part of an elephant's body is its trunk? (b)

2. Which animals can be trained to work for man? (c)

3. What is the range of an African male elephant's weight? (c)

4. Which of the following best describes the Asian elephant in comparison with the African elephant? (c)

5. Which is true of both elephants? (d)

6. Elephants use their trunks to pick up both small and large objects. (I heard it.)

7. Elephants enjoy working and doing tricks for people. (I cannot infer it.)

8. African elephants are generally more dangerous than Asian elephants. (I can infer it.)

9. Asian elephants like people more than African elephants do. (I cannot infer it.)

10. Some Asian elephants have tusks. (I can infer it.)

B. The Listening Expansion

Task 1.

Completing a Sketch

Let me tell you some more differences between my sisters, Alice and Betty. First of all, Betty wears glasses, but Alice does not. Alice has better eyesight than Betty. For another thing, Betty likes to wear a lot of jewelry—you know, necklaces, earrings, and rings. Today she's wearing two necklaces and a pair of earrings. Alice, on the other hand, usually doesn't wear any jewelry except a wedding ring. She wears a wedding ring because she's married. Betty doesn't wear a wedding ring. She's not married. She's single. Alice, however, is a wife and a mother. She has a young baby named Johnnie. Johnnie is asleep in his crib. Can you draw Johnnie asleep in his crib? I'll pause for a minute to let you draw Johnnie sleeping in his crib. Betty doesn't have any children. She does have pets, however. She has a little yellow bird. It's a canary. Draw Betty's canary in its cage. Betty also has a big cat named Brutus. Brutus would probably eat the canary if he could get into the cage. Draw Brutus, but don't draw him near the cage. Alice, unlike Betty, does not like animals in the house. On the other hand, she does like to have plants in the house. She has one very large house plant she especially likes. See the empty flower pot in the picture. Put a large plant into the pot.

There are many other differences between Betty and Alice, but that's all I'll tell you about right now.

Task 2.

Listening to a Dictation

1. Both Charles and David work in an office.

2. Both of my brothers are married.

3. Charles has two children, and David does, too.

4. David likes to play golf, and so does Charles.

5. The two of them have very similar lifestyles.

Listening Factoid #1

In the early 1970s five baby elephants were released in Kruger National Park in South Africa near a herd of buffalo. Park rangers later reported that one of the young elephants had joined the herd of buffalo and was acting like a buffalo. A visitor to the park in 1980 saw the ten-year-old elephant with its adopted family of about 20 buffalo. The buffalo and the elephant were trying to chase some lions away from a water hole. A few years later a park ranger reported seeing the young elephant and the herd of buffalo drinking water from a water hole when a herd of elephants arrived to drink water. The herd of buffalo ran off when they saw the herd of elephants, and the young elephant ran off along with the herd of buffalo. It appears that the elephant was accepted as a member of the herd by the buffalo.

Listening Factoid #2

An elephant grasps objects with its trunk much as a person does with a hand. The elephant's trunk can carry a log that weighs as much as 600 pounds (or 272 kilograms). The tip of the trunk can pick up an object as small as a coin. An elephant also uses its trunk to communicate with other elephants. When two elephants greet each other, each places the tip of its trunk in the other's mouth. A mother will comfort her calf by stroking it with her trunk. Young males also play-fight by wrestling with their trunks.

Unit Four/Focus on: Comparison/Contrast

Chapter 11 Lincoln and Kennedy: Similar Destinies

II. LISTENING

A. Initial Listening

John F. Kennedy and Abraham Lincoln lived in different times and had very different family and educational *backgrounds*. Kennedy lived in the 20th *century*; Lincoln lived in the 19th century. Kennedy was born in 1917, whereas Lincoln was born more than a hundred years earlier, in 1809. As for their family backgrounds, Kennedy came from a rich family, but Lincoln's family was not wealthy. Because Kennedy came from a wealthy family, he was able to attend expensive private schools. He graduated from Harvard University. Lincoln, on the other hand, had only one year of *formal schooling*. In spite of his lack of formal schooling, he became a well-known lawyer. He taught himself law by reading law books. Lincoln was, in other words, a self-educated man.

In spite of these differences in Kennedy and Lincoln's backgrounds, some interesting similarities between the two men are evident. In fact, books have been written about the strange *coincidences* in the lives of these two men. For example, take their political careers. Lincoln began his political career as a *congressman*. Similarly, Kennedy also began his political career as a congressman. Lincoln was elected to the *U.S. House of Representatives* in 1847, and Kennedy was elected to *the House* in 1947. They went to *Congress* just 100 years apart. Another interesting coincidence is that each man was elected president of the United States in a year ending with the number 60. Lincoln was elected president in 1860, and Kennedy was elected in 1960; furthermore, both men were president during years of *civil unrest* in the country. Lincoln was president during *the American Civil War*. During Kennedy's term of office, civil unrest took the form of *civil rights demonstrations*.

Another striking similarity between the two men was that, as you probably know, neither president lived to complete his term in office. Lincoln and Kennedy were both *assassinated* while in office. Kennedy was assassinated in Dallas, Texas, after only 1,000 days in office. Lincoln was assassinated in 1865 a few days after the end of *the American Civil War*. It is rather curious to note that both presidents were shot while they were sitting next to their wives.

These are only a few examples of the uncanny, or unusual similarities in the *destinies* of these two Americans—men who had a tremendous *impact* on the social and political life in the United States and the imagination of the American people.

B. Mental Rehearsal and Review of the Talk

Kennedy and Lincoln lived in different times.
They had different family and educational backgrounds.
Kennedy lived in the 20th century.
Lincoln lived in the 19th century.
Kennedy was born in 1917.
Lincoln was born in 1809.
Kennedy came from a wealthy family.
He went to expensive private schools.
He graduated from Harvard University.
Lincoln had only one year of formal schooling.
He taught himself law and became a lawyer.
He was a self-educated man.
There are many coincidences in the lives of the two men.
Lincoln began his political career as a congressman.
Kennedy began his political career as a congressman.
Lincoln was elected to the Congress in 1847.
Kennedy was elected to the Congress in 1947.
Lincoln was elected president in 1860.
Kennedy was elected president in 1960.
Lincoln and Kennedy were presidents during years of civil unrest.
Lincoln was president during the Civil War.
During Kennedy's term there were civil rights demonstrations.
Neither lived to complete his presidency.
Lincoln was assassinated in 1865.
Kennedy was assassinated in 1963 in Dallas, Texas.
Kennedy and Lincoln had a tremendous impact on the social and political life of the United States.
They had an impact on the imagination of the American people.

C. Consolidation

See II. A.

III. POSTLISTENING

A. The Comprehension Check

1. Recognizing Information and Checking Accuracy

A variety of answers are possible. Here are some sample responses.

1. In what century was Lincoln born? (the 19th century)

2. Why was Kennedy able to attend expensive private schools? (because his family was rich)

3. How many years did Lincoln attend school? (one year)

4. How did Lincoln get most of his education? (by reading books at home)

5. How did both Kennedy and Lincoln begin their political careers? (as congressmen; as members of the U.S. House of Representatives)

6. When was Kennedy elected president? (in 1960)

7. During which American war was Lincoln president? (during the American Civil War)

8. How did both Kennedy and Lincoln die? (by assassination; they were assassinated)

9. How long was Kennedy president of the United States? (1,000 days)

10. When was Lincoln murdered? (in 1865; a few days after the end of the Civil War)

B. The Listening Expansion

Task 1.   **A Dictation on Similarities**

1. Both women were 24 years old when they married.

2. Neither of the women was interested in politics.

3. Both were socially prominent women who spoke French.

4. Both Mrs. Lincoln and Mrs. Kennedy suffered the death of a child.

5. Neither Mrs. Kennedy nor Mrs. Lincoln was injured by the assassin.

Task 2.   **Detecting Similarities and Differences**

1. Andrew Johnson was a large man, and so was Lyndon Johnson. (similarity)

2. Neither of the vice presidents was from the North. (similarity)

3. Lyndon Johnson was later elected president of the United States, whereas Andrew Johnson was not. (difference)

4. Andrew Johnson had 13 letters in his name, and Lyndon Johnson did, also. (similarity)

5. Kennedy's vice president was born in the 19th century while Lincoln was born in the 18th century. (difference)

Listening Factoid #1

Lincoln issued the Emancipation Proclamation during the Civil War. The Proclamation freed the slaves, but only those in the Confederate States. It did not free the slaves living in Kentucky, Maryland, and the other slave-holding states that fought on the side of the North. Why then is Lincoln called "The Great Emancipator"? He deserves to be called "The Great Emancipator" not because of this 1863 proclamation, but because he urged Congress to adopt the Thirteenth Amendment, which abolished slavery in the United States. The amendment was passed by the American Congress in 1865.

Listening Factoid #2

Most of you would probably not be very surprised to learn that there was someone else at the party with your exact birthday if there were 365 people at the party. But how about if there were only 30 people? Do you think it would be likely that there would be another person at the party with the same birthday as yours? Well, actually, you would have a 50% chance of meeting someone with your exact birthday if there were only *23* people at the party! This is surprising to most people, and when it happens, it seems like a remarkable coincidence, but, in fact, it is simply a statistical probability.

Chapter 12   The *Titanic* and the *Andrea Doria*: Tragedies at Sea

II. LISTENING

A. Initial Listening

On the morning of April 10, 1912, the *luxury liner* the *Titanic* left England on a voyage to New York. Four days later, she lay at the bottom of the Atlantic Ocean. On Wednesday, July 18, 1956, the ocean liner the *Andrea Doria* left Italy. The *Andrea Doria* was also traveling to New York. Eight days later this great ship also lay at the bottom of the Atlantic.

The sinking of these two huge ships, these two very, very large ships, *shocked* the world. Reports of these two *tragedies* filled the newspapers for days. When the *Andrea Doria* went down, people compared her sinking with the sinking of the *Titanic*. There were similarities between the two events; however, there were also important differences.

What were some of these similarities? First of all, both ships were transatlantic ocean liners. In addition, they were also both luxury liners. They carried many of the world's rich and famous people. In fact, ten American millionaires lost their lives when the *Titanic* went down. Today millions of dollars worth of gold, silver, and cash may still remain locked inside these two sunken ships.

Another similarity was that, as each ship was sinking, there were acts of *heroism* and acts of *villainy*. Some people acted very bravely, even heroically. Some people even gave up their lives so that others could live. There were also some people who acted like *cowards*. For example, one man on the *Titanic* dressed up as a woman so that he could get into a lifeboat and save his own life. One last similarity was that both of these ships were considered "unsinkable." People believed that they would never sink.

I'd like to shift my attention now to the differences between these great ship *disasters*. To begin with, the *Titanic* was on her maiden voyage; that is, she was on her very first voyage across the Atlantic. The *Andrea Doria*, on the other hand, was on her 101st transatlantic crossing. Another difference was that the ships sank for different reasons. The *Titanic* struck an *iceberg* whereas the *Andrea Doria collided with* another ship. Another contrast was that the *Andrea Doria* had radar to warn of the approach of another ship, but the *Titanic* was not equipped with radar. The *Titanic* had only a *lookout*. The lookout was able to see the iceberg only moments before the ship struck it. But, of course, the greatest difference between these two terrible accidents was the number of lives lost. When the *Titanic* sank, more than 1,500 people died. They drowned or froze to death in the icy North Atlantic water. Over 700 people *survived* the sinking of the *Titanic*. In the *Andrea Doria* accident 60 people lost their lives, and about 1,650 lives were saved. One of the reasons that so many people died on the *Titanic* was that the ship was considered to be unsinkable, and so there were about half the number of lifeboats needed to *rescue* all the people aboard the ship. The *Andrea Doria* had more than enough lifeboats to rescue every person on the ship; however, they were able to use only about half of the lifeboats they had because of a mechanical problem. The passengers and *crew* of the *Andrea Doria* were very lucky that another ship was able to rescue most of them. The passengers on the *Titanic* were not so fortunate. It is interesting that the wreck of the *Titanic* was only found in September of 1985.

Whenever there are large numbers of people traveling together on a boat, ship, or plane, the possibility of disaster is always present. Most people arrive safely at their destination, but accidents like shipwrecks and plane crashes do happen, and these accidents remind us that no matter how safe we feel, accidents can happen suddenly and unexpectedly.

B. Mental Rehearsal and Review of the Talk

On April 10, 1912, the *Titanic* left England.
The *Titanic* left for New York.
Four days later she was at the bottom of the ocean.
On July 18, 1956, the *Andrea Doria* left Italy.
She was also traveling to New York.
Eight days later she was at the bottom of the Atlantic.
The sinking of these two ships shocked the world.
Reports filled the newspapers for days.
People compared the *Andrea Doria* with the *Titanic*.
There were similarities between the two events.
There were also differences.
What were the similarities?
Both were transatlantic ocean liners.
Both were luxury liners.
They carried many rich, famous people.
Millions of dollars remain inside the ships.
There were acts of heroism and villainy.
Both ships were considered unsinkable.
There were differences between the ship disasters.
The *Titanic* was on her maiden voyage.
The *Andrea Doria* was on her 101st crossing.
The ships sank for different reasons.
The *Titanic* struck an iceberg.
The *Andrea Doria* collided with another ship.
The *Andrea Doria* had radar.
The *Titanic* had only a lookout.
There was a difference in the number of lives lost.
More than 1,500 people died on the *Titanic*.
Over 700 people survived.
Sixty people died on the *Andrea Doria*.
One thousand six hundred fifty lives were saved.

There were about half the needed lifeboats on the *Titanic*.
The *Andrea Doria* had enough lifeboats.
But they were able to use only half of the lifeboats.
Another ship rescued most of the passengers and crew.
Whenever people travel, there is a possibility of disaster.

C. Consolidation

See II. A.

III. POSTLISTENING

A. The Comprehension Check

1. Recognizing Information and Checking Accuracy

1. What was the destination of the *Titanic* as it was sailing across the Atlantic? (c)

2. How were the *Titanic* and the *Andrea Doria* similar? (d)

3. How were the *Titanic* and the *Andrea Doria* different? (b)

4. Dressing up as a woman to save your life is an example of which of the following? (c)

5. What was different about the sinking of the *Andrea Doria* from the sinking of the *Titanic*? (b)

6. Fewer people on the *Titanic* would have died if there had been more lifeboats available. (I can infer it.)

7. The *Andrea Doria* was crossing the Atlantic for the 101st time. (I heard it.)

8. More people on the *Andrea Doria* would have died if there hadn't been another ship near by to rescue most of the people. (I can infer it.)

9. It's very dangerous to travel the Atlantic by ship. (I cannot infer it.)

10. The *Titanic* struck an iceberg, but the *Andrea Doria* collided with another ship. (I heard it.)

11. The radar system on the *Andrea Doria* was not working when the two ships collided. (I cannot infer it.)

B. The Listening Expansion

Task 1. **A Dramatization**

SS: Did you hear any cries of distress?
OP: Oh, yes.
SS: What were they—cries for help?
OP: Crying, shouting, moaning.

SS: From the ship or from the water?

OP: From the water, after the ship disappeared—no noises before. . . .

SS: Did you attempt to get near them?

OP: As soon as she disappeared, I said "Now, men, we will pull toward the wreck." Everyone in my boat said it was a mad idea, because we had far better save what few we had in my boat than go back to the scene of the wreck and be swamped by the crowds that were there.

SS: Tell us about your fellow passengers on that lifeboat. You say they discouraged you from returning or going in the direction of these cries?

OP: They did. I told my men to get their oars out and pull toward the wreck—the scene of the wreck . . . I said, "We may be able to pick up a few more."

SS: Who demurred to that?

OP: The whole crowd in my boat. A great number of them did.

SS: Women?

OP: I couldn't discriminate whether women or men. They said it was rather a mad idea.

SS: I'll ask you if any woman in your boat appealed to you to return to the direction from which the cries came.

OP: No one.

SS: You say that no woman passenger in your boat urged you to return?

Charles Burlingham interrupts: It would have capsized the boat, Senator.

SS: Pardon me. I am not drawing any unfair conclusion from this. One of the officers told us that a woman in his boat urged him to return to the side of the ship. I want to be very sure that this officer heard no woman asking the same thing. Who demurred, now that you can specifically recall?

OP: I could not name anyone in particular.

SS: The men with the oars?

OP: No, they did not. No. They started to obey my orders.

SS: You were in command. They ought to have obeyed your orders.

OP: So they did.

SS: They did not—if you told them to pull toward the ship.

OP: They commenced pulling toward the ship, and the passengers in my boat said it was a mad idea on my part to pull back to the ship because if I did, we should be swamped with the crowd that was in the water, and it would add another 40 to the list of the drowned. And I decided I wouldn't pull back. . . .

SS: How many of these cries were there?

OP: I'd rather you didn't speak about that.

SS: I would like to know how you were impressed by it.

OP: Well, I can't very well describe it. I'd rather you not speak of it.

SS: I realize that it isn't a pleasant theme, and yet I would like to know whether these cries were general and in a chorus or desultory and occasional?

OP: There was a continual moan for about an hour.

SS: And you lay in the vicinity of that scene for about an hour?

OP: Oh, *please*, sir, don't! I cannot bear to recall it. I wish we might not discuss the scene!

SS: I have no desire to lacerate your feelings. But we must know whether you drifted in the vicinity of that scene for about an hour.

OP: Oh, yes, we were in the vicinity of the wreck the whole time. . . .

SS: Did this anguish or these cries of distress die away?

OP: Yes, they did—they died away gradually.

SS: Did they continue during most of the hour?

OP: Oh, yes—I think so. It may have been a shorter time—of course I didn't watch every five minutes!

SS: I understand that, and I am not trying to ask about a question of five minutes. Is that all you care to say?

OP: I'd rather you'd have left that out altogether.

SS: I know you would, but I must know what efforts you made to save the lives of passengers and crew under your charge. If that is all the effort you made, say so and I will stop that branch of my examination.

OP: That is all, sir! That's all the effort I made.

Task 2.

Deciding Whether You Agree or Disagree With Stated Opinions

1. Senator Smith thought that Officer Pitman should have gone back for more people who were still in the water.

2. If Officer Pitman had gone back for the people in the water, he would have been putting the people already in his boats in danger.

3. Officer Pitman made the right decision not to go back for the people in the water.

4. Senator Smith was not sympathetic to Officer Pitman.

5. Officer Pitman was telling the truth.

6. It was the fault of the women on the boat that Officer Pitman did not go back to pick up the people in the water.

7. Officer Pitman was not sure that he had made the right decision not to return to pick up more people.

8. Officer Pitman was still very upset by what had happened.

9. You would have acted differently if you had been Officer Pitman.

10. It's difficult for anyone to know how he or she would act in a terrible situation like the sinking of the *Titanic*.

11. Officer Pitman acted like a villain and a coward.

Listening Factoid #1

In a recent survey reported in the Pittsburgh *Post-Gazette*, American men were asked if they would give up their seats to other people if they were on the *Titanic* today. Seventy-four percent of the men said they would give up their seat in a lifeboat for their child. Almost as many men, 67%, said they would surrender their seat to their wife. Fifty-four percent reported that they would give their seat to their mother, and 52% said they would for their father. Only 35% said they would give up their seat to any other woman who was not a wife or a child. However, 52% said they would give up their seat for the Catholic humanitarian Mother Teresa, but only 8% said they would give up their seat to pop singer Madonna.

Listening Factoid #2

The story of the ill-fated *Titanic* continues to interest people today partly because of the 1998 Hollywood movie, *Titanic*. People are also still interested because of the discovery of where the *Titanic* lies at the bottom of the Atlantic Ocean. In 1986, Robert Ballard and a group of scientists located the resting place of the *Titanic* beneath 12,000 feet, or 3,647 meters, of water in the north Atlantic.

Since Ballard's discovery of the resting place of the *Titanic*, a number of scientific and commercial expeditions have visited the site, and more than 8,000 artifacts have been taken (or stolen) from the sunken ship. These artifacts include jewelry, dishes and glasses, and many other things that went down with the ship.

Various companies have taken tourists in submarines to visit the *Titanic*. Some of the submarines have landed on the deck of the sunken ship, and left holes in the deck of the *Titanic*.

Scientists have determined that the wreck of the *Titanic* has deteriorated significantly since its 1986 discovery for two reasons: (1) natural forces; and (2) underwater tourists and treasure hunters.

It is estimated that by the year 2004, more than 200 tourists had visited the *Titanic* in submarines. Treasure hunters had also visited in submarines and taken thousands of artifacts or treasures from the ship. In fact, in 2003, a menu taken from the *Titanic* sold for 25,000 euros at an auction, and one of the *Titanic*'s deck chairs went for 30,000 euros.

Everyone seems to want a piece of the *Titanic*, and a piece of history.

Unit Five/Focus on: Causal Analysis

Chapter 13   Dinosaurs: Why They Disappeared

II. LISTENING

A. Initial Listening

Several *theories* have been *proposed* about why the dinosaurs disappeared from the face of the earth. In recent years one popular theory proposes that climatic changes caused the dinosaurs to *become extinct*. This climatic change theory says that millions of years ago the climate of the world gradually became colder. As the earth slowly became colder, fewer plants were able to grow. The cold weather finally resulted in a *severe* shortage of food for the dinosaurs. As you probably know, most of the dinosaurs were vegetarians, and they depended on plants for their food supply. In summary, then, the disappearance of the dinosaurs was caused directly by a shortage of plants to eat, and indirectly by a change in the climate. Many scientists still believe that the climatic change theory best explains why the dinosaurs disappeared. This theory argues that the dinosaurs disappeared gradually—slowly—as the earth became colder and as their food supply *dwindled*.

Today there is new *evidence* for the theory that the dinosaurs did not disappear gradually, but that they disappeared quickly and suddenly. This theory is known as the *asteroid* theory. It states that a huge asteroid, or perhaps a *comet*, hit the earth about 65 million years ago. When this comet or asteroid hit the earth, it caused a huge dust cloud. The huge dust cloud covered the whole earth and *blocked out the sun* for months. Since there was no sun for many, many months, most of the plants on earth died. The dinosaur's food supply was destroyed in a period of months.

While this asteroid theory is not new, what is new is the evidence for the theory. Until recently there was no evidence that an asteroid or a comet had hit the earth 65 million years ago. What happened recently was that scientists found large amounts of a *rare earth element* called iridium all over the world. This iridium was found in *layers of the earth* that are 65 million years old. The iridium was found in the same layers where the bones of the last dinosaurs were found.

The element iridium is very uncommon, in fact, rare, on the earth. It is an element, however, that is more often found in space. Scientists *speculate* that this iridium was brought to earth 65 million years ago when a comet or asteroid hit the earth.

The comet or asteroid theory explains two things: (1) It explains the larger amounts of the rare element iridium found in the 65-million-year-old layers of earth, and (2) it explains why the dinosaurs disappeared from the earth.

Today scientists continue to *debate* the two theories: the climatic change theory and the asteroid theory. In the future evidence may be found that supports a totally new theory of why the terrible *lizards* died out.

B. Mental Rehearsal and Review of the Talk

There are several theories why the dinosaurs disappeared.
One theory is the climatic change theory.
Climatic changes caused the dinosaurs to become extinct.
Sixty-five million years ago the climate slowly got colder.
Fewer plants were able to grow.
The cold weather resulted in a severe food shortage for the dinosaurs.
Most dinosaurs were vegetarians.
They depended on plants for food.
The disappearance was directly caused by a shortage of food.
The disappearance was indirectly caused by climatic changes.
According to the climatic change theory, the dinosaurs disappeared slowly.
They disappeared slowly as their food supply dwindled.
There is new evidence for the asteroid theory.
According to the asteroid theory, the dinosaurs disappeared suddenly.
An asteroid or a comet hit the earth 65 million years ago.
The asteroid or comet caused a huge dust cloud.
The dust cloud blocked the sun for months.
The dinosaurs' food supply was destroyed.
Most of the plants on earth died in a few months.
The dinosaurs died very quickly.
The asteroid theory is not new.
The evidence for the theory is new.
Scientists found large amounts of iridium all over the world.
The iridium was found in layers of earth.
The layers of earth are 65 million years old.
The bones of the last dinosaurs are found in the same layers.
Iridium is rare on earth.
Iridium is more common in space.
An asteroid or comet may have brought the iridium to earth.
Scientists continue to debate the two theories.
In the future, evidence may be found for a new theory.

C. Consolidation

See II. A.

III. POSTLISTENING

A. The Comprehension Check

1. Recognizing Information and Checking Accuracy

1. What does the statement "Dinosaurs are extinct" mean? (d)

2. Why did the dinosaurs die out, according to the asteroid theory? (d)

3. Which of the following statements is true, according to the climatic change theory? (b)

4. Which of the following statements is true? (b)

5. The climatic change theory says that cold weather caused a serious shortage of food for the dinosaurs. (I heard it.)

6. According to the asteroid theory, a dust cloud caused the plants to die. (I heard it.)

7. Fewer plants are able to grow when the weather is cold. (I can infer it.)

8. Some dinosaurs were over 100 feet tall. (I cannot infer it.)

9. Larger amounts of iridium can be found in space than on earth. (I heard it.)

10. If the asteroid theory is correct, the earth was dark, day and night, for several months. (I can infer it.)

B. The Listening Expansion

Task 1.   **Recognizing Possible Causes of a Situation**

1. My TV set isn't working. What is wrong with it? (a) (b) (d)

2. Mary doesn't want to go to the picnic today. Why doesn't she want to go? (b) (d)

3. The launching of the spacecraft was postponed until tomorrow. What might have caused the postponement? (a) (c) (d)

4. John was fired from his job at the bank. Why might he have been fired? (a) (c)

5. John was born in Paris, France, in 1940. Why was he born in Paris? (d)

6. All of the students in the class passed the examination except Mary. How come? (b) (d)

7. You are trying to call your doctor, but nobody answers the phone. What's the reason she's not answering your call? (a) (b) (c) (d)

8. John lost a lot of money gambling in Monte Carlo. Why? (a)

9. Mary decided not to marry John. Why did she make that decision? (a) (d)

10. John is wearing tennis clothes and carrying a tennis racket. Why is John dressed in those clothes? (b)

Task 2.   **Predicting the End of a Story: Stating the Possible Results**

1. It's a cold and snowy night. A man and a woman are traveling in a car. They are driving along a winding mountain road. It is difficult to see out the windshield because the snow is falling so hard and because one of the windshield wipers is broken. Suddenly there is

a sharp curve in the road. The man steps on the brakes hard. What happens?

2. It's the last half of a championship soccer game. The team from France has scored three goals. The team from Venezuela has scored three goals. The score is 3 to 3. Suddenly the forward on the French team gets the ball. He takes it toward the French goal. He's close to the goal. He kicks the ball. What happens?

3. A man is walking along the river. Suddenly he hears a young boy calling for help. The man looks toward the river and sees a young boy. The boy is trying to stay on top of the water. The man is not a good swimmer. What happens?

4. You and your friend Bob are sitting in the movie theater waiting for the movie to begin. Bob is telling you about his girlfriend Donna. He says that Donna told him that she had to visit a friend who is sick this evening. Then you and Bob see Donna and another man walking down the aisle. They are looking for seats. They don't see Bob and you. Bob suddenly stands up and says to you, "Excuse me for a minute." What happens?

5. You are waiting in line at the bank to cash a check. You hear a woman scream. You turn around and see three men with guns in their hands and masks on their faces. One of the men yells for everyone to lie down on the floor. You lie down on the floor quickly. What happens?

Listening Factoid #1

Dinosaurs are generally believed to have been very large animals and it's true that *some* of them were incredibly large. One dinosaur, believed to have been the largest dinosaur ever, is called *seismosaurus*. *Seismosaurus* literally means "earth shaker." This animal was between 100 and 120 feet long and weighed about 89 tons. To give you some idea of how big *seismosaurus* was, let me tell you that an American football field is 300 feet long. Consider that the African elephant weighs between six and seven tons. This means that *seismosaurus* was about 13 to 14 times heavier than an African elephant. It's not surprising that his name means "earth shaker"!

Listening Factoid #2

Dinosaur life spans probably varied in length from *tens* of years to *hundreds* of years. Many scientists who study dinosaurs think that their possible age can be estimated from the maximum life spans of modern reptiles, such as the 66-year lifespan of the common alligator and the amazing lifespan of a Black Seychelles Tortoise. The Black Seychelles Tortoise is now extinct, but one of these tortoises was captured in 1766, when it was an adult tortoise. The captured tortoise lived until 1918, a record 152 years in captivity. The sad thing is that the tortoise had an accidental death, so no one knows how long it might have lived, if it had not been for the accident. Now, these estimates of the life spans of the dinosaurs would be too long if it turned out that dinosaurs were more similar to modern birds or animals, rather than to reptiles, as some scientists believe. Scientists may gain more knowledge about the life spans of the dinosaurs in coming years.

Unit Five/Focus on: Causal Analysis

Chapter 14 The American Civil War: Why It Happened

II. LISTENING

A. Initial Listening

The American Civil War was fought over 100 years ago. It began in 1861 and lasted until 1865. The battles of the American Civil War resulted in the death of 620,000 Americans. What caused this terrible civil war between the North and the South?

Well, historians believe that there were many causes of the war. One of the important causes of the war was the *friction* between the North and the South over the issue of slavery. The southern way of life and the southern economy were based on the use of slave labor. For almost 250 years before the Civil War, the economy of the South depended on the use of black slaves. The slaves were used to plant and pick cotton and tobacco. Cotton and tobacco were the main crops grown in the South. Most Southerners did not think it was wrong to own, buy, or sell slaves like farm animals. Slavery was, in fact, the *foundation* of the entire economy and way of life in the South. This was not the situation in the North. The northern economy did not depend on the use of slave labor. Why not?

Well, in the South there were many large cotton *plantations* that used hundreds of slaves. In the North, however, there were smaller farms. The northern farmers planted many different kinds of crops, not just cotton or tobacco. The Northerners did not need slaves, since their farms were smaller than most of the southern plantations. In fact, many Northerners were so opposed to slavery that they wanted to end slavery completely. The northern *attitude* against slavery made the Southerners angry. So, for many years before the war, there was constant friction between the North and the South over this issue. This friction eventually led to war.

There was other friction, too, as I said before, between the North and the South. There were, in other words, other causes of *conflict* between the North and the South. One involved the growth of industry in the North. While the South remained an agricultural area, the North became more and more industrialized. As industry increased in the North, it brought more people and greater wealth to the northern states. As a result, many Southerners began to fear northern political and economic *domination*. Because of this fear, many Southerners believed that the South should leave *the Union* and that they should form their own country.

In 1860, the Southerners decided it was time to leave the Union when Abraham Lincoln became president of the United States. Lincoln, as you may know, was against slavery. The people of the South were afraid that their way of life and their economic system were in danger with Lincoln in the presidency. Consequently, the southern states decided to *secede* from the Union. In other words, they wanted to break away from the North and form a separate country. In 1861, South Carolina seceded, and by June of 1861 eleven southern states had seceded and established a new country. They called the new country the *Confederate States of America*. The war between the North and the South began when the southern states seceded from the Union.

The main reason that the North went to war against the South was to bring the southern states back into the Union. In other words, the North went to war to keep the United States one country.

After four years of terrible fighting, the North won the war against the South, and the United States remained one country. The North won the war mainly because of its economic and industrial strength and power.

The Civil War had two important results for the United States: (1) the Civil War *preserved* the United States as one country; and (2) it ended slavery in the United States.

Many Americans wonder what the United States would be like today if the South had won the Civil War. The history of the United States would have been very different if the South had won the war between the States.

B. Mental Rehearsal and Review of the Talk

The American Civil War was fought over 100 years ago.
The Civil War began in 1861.
The war lasted until 1865.
War battles resulted in the death of about 620,000 Americans.
What caused the Civil War between the North and the South?
There were many causes of the war.
One cause was the issue of slavery.
The southern way of life was based on slave labor.
The economy of the South depended on slaves for 250 years.
Slaves planted and picked cotton and tobacco.
Southerners owned, bought, and sold slaves.
Southerners did not think this was wrong.
Slavery was the foundation of the southern economy.
The northern economy did not depend on slave labor.
In the South, there were many large cotton plantations.
These plantations used hundreds of black slaves.
In the North, there were smaller farms.
The northern farmers planted many different crops.
Northerners did not need slaves on their small farms.
Many Northerners were opposed to slavery.
Many Northerners wanted to end slavery completely.
The northern attitude against slavery made Southerners angry.
There was constant friction between the North and the South.
The friction was over the issue of slavery.
The friction eventually led to war.

There were other frictions between the North and the South.
One friction involved the growth of industry in the North.
The South remained an agricultural area.
The North became more and more industrialized.
Industry brought people and wealth to the North.
Southerners began to fear northern political and economic domination.
Many Southerners wanted to leave the Union.
The Southerners wanted to form a separate country.
In 1860, Abraham Lincoln became president.
Lincoln was against slavery.
The southern states decided to secede from the Union.
In 1861, South Carolina seceded.
By June of 1861 eleven southern states had seceded.
The eleven southern states established a new country.
The new country was called the Confederate States of America.
The Civil War began when the southern states seceded from the Union.
The North went to war to bring the southern states into the Union.
After four years, the North won the war.
The North won the war because of its economic and industrial power.
The Civil War had two important results.
The Civil War preserved the United States as one country.
The Civil War ended slavery in the United States.
American history might have been different if the South had won.

C. Consolidation

See II. A.

III. POSTLISTENING

A. The Comprehension Check

1. Recognizing Information and Checking Accuracy

1. How long did the American Civil War last? (b)

2. What was one cause of the American Civil War? (b)

3. Describe the economy of the South at the time of the Civil War. (c)

4. How was the economy of the North different from the economy of the South before the war? (d)

5. How did the growth of industry change the North? (b)

6. Why did the South decide to leave the Union and form its own country? (b)

7. What was the name of the country formed by the southern states? (d)

8. What was the most important reason that the North went to war with the South? (b)

9. Why did the North win the war? (d)

10. What did the Civil War accomplish? (c)

11. The American Civil War started in 1861. (T)

12. The American Civil War ended over 100 years ago. (T)

13. There were many large cotton plantations in the North before the war. (F There were many large cotton plantations in the South.)

14. The use of slaves in the South began around the time of the American Civil War. (F For almost 250 years before the Civil War, the economy of the South depended on the use of slaves.)

15. Most Southerners felt that it was all right to own, buy, and sell slaves. (T)

16. Most slaves were unhappy and wanted President Lincoln to free them. (?)

17. Most Northerners wanted to use slaves to work on their small farms. (F The Northerners did not need slaves on their small farms.)

18. The only reason for the American Civil War was the issue of slavery. (F There were other causes of the conflict between the North and the South, for example, the growth of industry in the North.)

19. The North had better soldiers and generals than the South did. (?)

20. The American Civil War was over in a few months. (F The war lasted from 1861 to 1865.)

B. The Listening Expansion

Task 1.　　　　**A Listening Dictation**

1. The South lost the war because it had fewer men and far fewer supplies.

2. The South could not ship supplies to its soldiers since it did not have many railroads.

3. The North won the war as a result of its industrial power.

4. The soldiers of the South suffered because of a lack of food.

5. The greater number of soldiers in the North was due to the fact that it had a larger population.

Task 2.　　　　**Guessing Possible Causes of Events**

2. A student has just arrived at L.A. International Airport. He is waiting at the place were the luggage arrives. He has been waiting for a long time. He still hasn't seen his suitcases. What are some possible reasons he has not been able to find his luggage?

(Maybe he is waiting at the wrong place. Perhaps his luggage is lost. His luggage might be a little late arriving. Maybe he doesn't recognize his bags. Somebody might have taken his luggage by mistake. It's possible that someone has stolen his bags, etc.)

3. A man has just come home from work. He doesn't say hello to his wife. He goes directly into the living room and turns on the TV. He looks very angry. His wife asks him, "What's wrong?" He replies, "Nothing. Leave me alone." Why is the man angry? What happened at work that might have upset the man?

(Maybe he had a fight with his boss or one of his coworkers. He is very tired today and just wants to rest before dinner. The traffic on the way home was terrible. He got fired from his job. He is angry with his wife because . . . .)

4. Professor Jones is lecturing to her class. Suddenly she stops talking. She goes to the window and opens it. She stands at the window for a few minutes. Then she turns and leaves the room very quickly. She doesn't say anything to her students, but the door slams loudly when she leaves the room. Two students who were sleeping in the back of the room wake up and are very surprised that the professor has left. What are some possible reasons for the professor's behavior?

(The professor is sick. She saw something outside the building that she needed to do something about. What could that be? She is angry with the students who were sleeping in class, etc.)

5. You see a man in front of an expensive jewelry store in a large city. He is walking back and forth in front of the store. He looks into the store when he passes the door. From time to time he looks at his watch. He looks up and down the street nervously. He appears very upset. What are some possible causes for his nervousness?

(He is waiting for someone who is late. He can't decide if he wants to go into the store to buy his wife an expensive piece of jewelry or not. He is planning to rob the store and he's waiting for a good time to do it, etc.)

6. Your roommate has just opened a letter from home. She reads the letter, drops it on the floor, and starts to laugh and dance around the room. Why is she so happy?

(Her family sent her money to return home for a short vacation. Someone in her family is coming to visit her. One of her family or friends has had some good fortune. What is it?)

Listening Factoid #1

In 1853, a very important book against slavery was written by a woman who hated slavery. Her name was Harriet Beecher Stowe, and the title of the book was *Uncle Tom's Cabin*. The book quickly sold 100,000 copies; it helped create a wave of hatred against slavery in the North. When asked why she wrote it, Stowe stated that she had not written the book. She said, "God wrote it. I merely wrote his dictation." *Uncle Tom's Cabin* contributed to the start of the Civil War between the North and the South. In fact, when Abraham Lincoln met Harriet Beecher Stowe, he asked, "Is this the little woman whose book made such a great war?"

Listening Factoid #2

More men died in the Civil War than in all other wars fought by the United States before or since that time. 620,000 men died of wounds and disease during the Civil War. In the 3 days of the battle at Gettysburg, in Pennsylvania, 51,116 men lost their lives. It's also known that 3,000 horses were killed at Gettysburg.

Did you know that during the Battle of Gettysburg, in Pennsylvania, the only *civilian* to die was 20-year-old Mary Virginia Wade, who was shot through the heart while making bread?

It is known that 3,530 Native Americans fought for the North (or the Union). One-third, or 1,018, of these Native Americans lost their lives.

Did you know that when a woman mourned for a husband who died in the 1860s, she spent a minimum of two-and-a-half years in mourning? That meant little or no social activities: no parties, no outings, no visitors, and a wardrobe that consisted of nothing but black. However, the husband, when mourning for his wife who died, spent only three months in a black suit.

Did you know that during the Civil War, including the times before and after, it was legal and socially acceptable for a man to beat his wife, provided the instrument used in the beating was no thicker than his thumb? Thus, we get the term: Rule of thumb.

Unit Five/Focus on: Causal Analysis

Chapter 15   Endangered Species: What Are The Causes?

II. LISTENING

A. Initial Listening

Over the history of the earth, millions of animal and plant species have disappeared. Most of these species disappeared, or became extinct, because of natural causes such as climatic changes or a catastrophic event, like an asteroid hitting earth. What is different today is that most species that are in danger of becoming extinct are not endangered because of natural causes but because of human activity. Today, we will be looking at the reasons that many plants and animals are endangered and how these reasons, or causes, are related to human activity.

The single most important cause of endangered species today is the *destruction* and/or *degradation* of *habitat*. Most animals and plants are adapted to live and reproduce in a specific environment, or habitat. They cannot survive if they lose the specific habitat that they are adapted to live and reproduce in.

There are many ways that human activity destroys habitat. For example, forests, grasslands, and deserts, which provide habitat to many plants and animals, are cleared in order to develop residential areas for people to live in and industrial areas for people to work in. Land is also *cleared* to prepare it for farmers to grow crops on. *Swamps and marshes*, which provide habitat to many animal and plant species, are often *drained* and filled in, also to provide land for development or agriculture. In addition, rivers are sometimes *dammed* in order to provide people with electrical power. All of these human activities, such as clearing forests, grasslands, and deserts; draining swamps and marshes, and damming rivers result in the destruction of habitats that many plants and animals need to live and reproduce in.

Closely related to the destruction of habitat is the degradation of habitat, which also endangers many species. Some examples of manmade causes that degrade habitat are *oil spills, water pollution,* and *acid rain.* You probably have seen pictures in newspapers or on TV of dead or dying *marine animals* and birds covered with oil after an oil tanker accident. Human beings also cause water pollution, which endangers the survival of many fish and marine animals. Acid rain, which results from people burning fossil fuels, also harms many species of fish *and* many species of trees. To sum up, some of the things related to human activity that result in the degradation of the environment are oil spills, water pollution, and acid rain.

Illegal wildlife trade is the next major cause of endangered species. Although many governments have passed laws protecting endangered species, many animals are still illegally hunted. Sometimes people hunt these animals for food, but more often they hunt them only for specific parts of their bodies. For example, some species of animals such as tigers are illegally hunted for their furs. Elephants, which are the biggest land animals in the world and an endangered species, are often killed for their hides and tusks. These elephant hides and tusks are used to make souvenirs and works of art to sell to tourists and art collectors. Other animals such as chimpanzees are trapped to be sold to zoos for people to look at or for medical experiments. Some beautiful birds, such as some species of parrots, are in danger of extinction because so many are captured to be sold as pets to people all over the world.

The third major cause that many species are endangered is *over exploitation*. People have always exploited, or used, plants and animals, and will, no doubt, continue to do so. It is only when people exploit animals and plants in an excessive manner that they become endangered. Some animals have already been hunted to extinction for food and sometimes for sport. Let me give you one well-known example—the passenger pigeon in the United States. Passenger pigeons were once so plentiful that people said they darkened the sky for hours, even days, when they flew over the land. Many people thought that the passenger pigeon could never disappear, but, in reality, they became extinct at the beginning of the 20th century. They became extinct as a result of over hunting, partly for food but mostly for sport. Today, some fish, like the cod, which is an important source of food for people in many parts of the world, have been over fished. As a result, cod are in danger of becoming extinct. At one time cod, like passenger pigeons, were very plentiful, and it seemed they could never be gone. And it's not just animal species like the codfish that are in danger of becoming extinct. According to a recent article in the *New Scientist**, the Brazil nut tree, a very important source of nuts for both animals and people, is endangered due to over harvesting of the nuts.

The fourth and final reason that some species today are endangered has to do with competition that is directly related to human activity. As you know, most animal and plant species have *to compete* with other species in their habitat for food, water, and any other resources they both need. This is usually natural, that is, not related to human activity. However, some animal and plant species today also face competition that is directly related to human activity. There are two kinds of competition that animal and plant species can face that is related to human activity. One has to do with domestic animals and the other has to do with what is called "introduced" species. Let discuss competition with domestic animals first.

I'm sure you are all familiar with most domestic animals such as cattle, horses, sheep, goats, and so forth. But did you know that these domestic animals can be a threat to wild, that is, non-domestic, animals? The first reason is because these domestic animals compete for habitat with wild animals. And, in addition, the people who own these domestic animals often hunt, trap, and poison wild animals in

---

**New Scientist*, December 2003.

order to protect their livestock. The wolf is an example of an animal that is widely hunted to near extinction to protect domestic animals.

Another serious threat to some species is competition with introduced species, that is, plants or animals that are introduced, or brought, by humans into a new habitat, either on purpose or by accident. Take, for example, the introduction of a species of rabbit into Australia. In the 19th century, Europeans purposely introduced a species of European rabbit into Australia so they could hunt them for sport. Unfortunately, this animal has caused great damage to the habitat of many *native animals and plants* of Australia. Another introduced species, the brown tree snake, was accidentally introduced into the island of Guam in the late 1940s. These snakes accidentally rode along on military cargo planes that landed there. Since that time, the brown tree snake has destroyed a large part of the bird population of Guam.

Before I close, let me repeat the four major causes of endangered species today: (1) the destruction and/or degradation of habitat, (2) the illegal wildlife trade, (3) over exploitation, and (4) competition with domestic and "introduced" species.

Let me conclude by saying that the relationship of all living plants and animals is complex and interdependent. The destruction of one animal or plant species can threaten the survival of other species of animals and plants. Human beings are part of the natural world and they might also, one day, become an endangered species themselves. Because the four major causes of endangered species today are largely the result of human activity, only human beings can change the situation. Time *is running out* for many endangered plant and animal species.

B. Mental Rehearsal and Review of the Talk

Over the history of the earth, millions of species have disappeared.
Most of these species became extinct because of natural causes.
Natural causes include climatic changes and catastrophic events like an asteroid hitting earth.
Most species in danger of becoming extinct today are not endangered because of natural causes.
Today many species are endangered because of human activity.
We will look at the four major causes some animal and plants species are endangered.
These four major causes are related to human activity.
The single most important cause of endangered species today is the destruction and/or degradation of habitat.
Most animals and plants are adapted to live and reproduce in a specific habitat.
They cannot survive if they lose this specific habitat.
There are many ways that human activities destroy habitat.
Forests, grasslands, and deserts provide habitat to many plants and animals.

These lands are cleared to develop residential and industrial areas for people.

Land is also cleared for farmers to grow crops on.

Swamps and marshes provide habitat to many plant and animal species.

Swamps and marshes are drained and filled in to provide land for development or agriculture.

Rivers are sometimes dammed to provide people with electrical power.

Clearing land, draining swamps and marshes, and damming rivers are human activities.

All of these human activities result in the destruction of habitat.

The degradation of habitat is closely related to the destruction of habitat.

The degradation of habitat also endangers many species.

Some examples of manmade causes that degrade habitat are oil spills, water pollution, and acid rain.

You probably have seen pictures of dead or dying marine animals and birds covered with oil after an oil tanker accident.

Human beings cause water pollution.

Water pollution also endangers the survival of many species of fish and marine animals.

Acid rain results from people burning fossil fuels.

Acid rain harms many species of fish and many species of trees.

In sum, oil spills, water pollution, and acid rain are related to human activity.

Oil spills, water pollution, and acid rain degrade habitat and endanger some plant and animal species.

Illegal wildlife trade is the next major cause of endangered species.

Many governments have passed laws protecting endangered species.

Many animals are still illegally hunted.

Sometimes people hunt these animals for food.

More often people hunt these animals for specific parts of their bodies.

For example, tigers are illegally hunted for their furs.

Elephants are often killed for their hides and tusks.

Elephant hides and tusks are used to make souvenirs and works of art to sell.

Chimpanzees are trapped to be sold to zoos or for medical experiments.

Some beautiful birds, such as some species of parrots, are in danger of extinction.

These parrots are captured to be sold as pets.

The third major cause of endangered species is over exploitation.

People have always exploited, or used, plants and animals.

When plants and animals are exploited in an excessive manner, they become endangered.

Some animals have already been hunted to extinction for food or sport.

For example, the passenger pigeon in the United States was once very plentiful.

Many people thought that the passenger pigeon could never disappear.

Passenger pigeons became extinct at the beginning of the 20th century.

They became extinct as a result of over hunting, mostly for sport.

Today, some fish like the cod have been over fished.

The cod is an important source of food for people in many parts of the world.

At one time codfish, like passenger pigeons were very plentiful.

Today they are in danger of becoming extinct.

It's not just animal species that are in danger.

The Brazil nut tree is endangered due to over harvesting of the nuts.

The Brazil nut is an importance source of food for both animals and people.

The fourth and final reason that some species are endangered has to do with competition.

Most animal and plant species have to compete with other species in their habitat for food and water and other resources.

This kind of competition is natural.

It is not related to human activity.

Today some plant and animal species face two kinds of competition related to human activity.

The first kind of competition is with domestic animals.

The second kind of competition is with "introduced" species.

Let's discuss competition with domestic animals first.

Domestic animals include cattle, horses, sheep, goats, and so forth.

Did you know that domestic animals are a threat to many other species?

The first reason is because they compete for habitat with wild animals.

In addition, people also often hunt, trap, and poison wild animals to protect domestic animals.

Wolves have been hunted to near extinction to protect domestic animals.

The second kind of competition related to human activity is competition with "introduced" species.

Introduced species are plants or animals that are introduced by humans into a new habitat.

They are introduced either on purpose or by accident.

Europeans introduced a species of rabbit into Australia on purpose from Europe in the 19th century.

They introduced this species of rabbit as an animal to hunt for sport.

This rabbit has caused great damage to the habitat of many native animals and plants of Australia.

The brown tree snake was accidentally introduced into the island of Guam in the late 1940s.

The brown tree snake accidentally rode along on military cargo planes that landed there.

The brown tree snake has destroyed a large part of the bird population of Guam.

Let me repeat the four major causes of endangered species today.

Number 1 is the destruction and/or degradation of habitat.

Number 2 is the illegal wildlife trade.

Number 3 is over exploitation.

Number 4 is competition with domestic animals and with "introduced" species.

In conclusion, the relationship of all living plants and animals is complex and interdependent.

The destruction of one animal or plant species can threaten the survival of other species.
Human beings are part of the natural world.
Human beings could, one day, become an endangered species.
The four major causes of endangered species today are largely the result of human activity.
Time is running out for many endangered plant and animal species.
Only human beings can change the situation.

C. Consolidation

See II. A.

III. POSTLISTENING

A. The Comprehension Check

1. Recognizing Information and Checking Accuracy

1. What is the most important cause of endangered species today? (c)

2. Which of the following is *not* mentioned as an endangered species? (b)

3. Which of the following is an example of destruction of habitat? (d)

4. Which of the following is an example of degradation of habitat? (a)

5. Which of the following is an example of a domestic animal? (b)

6. Which of the following is a source of food for humans that is in danger of becoming extinct? (d)

7. Most of the causes that are endangering species today are related to human activity. (T)

8. Rivers are sometimes dammed to provide electrical power. (T)

9. The passenger pigeon is an endangered species. (F The passenger pigeon became extinct at the beginning of the 20th century.)

10. Some species are introduced into a new habitat on purpose and some are introduced by accident. (T)

11. The brown tree snake was introduced onto the island of Guam on purpose. (F The brown tree snake was accidentally introduced onto the island of Guam.)

12. For most of the history of the earth, human activity was *not* the most cause of endangered species. (I can infer it.)

13. The more human beings there are on earth, the more plant and animal species will be threatened. (I can infer it.)

14. Marine animals are threatened by oil spills and water pollution. (I heard it.)

15. Human beings will stop polluting water very soon. (I can't infer it.)

B. The Listening Expansion

Task 1. **Listening to Complete a Chart**

As you know, many, many animals and plants species all over the world are endangered. Many of these animals and plants are endangered for more than one reason. In your book there is a chart with five endangered animals and two endangered plants. The chart has the common name of the animals and plants, their habitats, or where they are found in nature, and the reasons they are endangered. Look at the Giant Panda in the chart. The Giant Panda is found in China. It is endangered as a result of habitat destruction, illegal killing for its fur, and illegal capture for zoos. Let's fill in the missing information—the information not in the chart—for the other animals and plants. Are you ready? OK, let's begin with the next animal on the chart—the blue whale. The blue whale is found in all oceans. It is endangered because it is over hunted for blubber, food, and whale oil. Write "all oceans" in the correct place. The next animal on the chart is the California condor, a very large and beautiful bird. It is found in the United States in Southern California and Arizona. It is endangered because its habitat is being destroyed, it is hunted for sport, and it is poisoned to protect domestic animals. Write "hunted for sport" in the correct place. Now let's look at the black rhinoceros, which is found south of the Sahara Desert in Africa. This animal is endangered due to habitat destruction and because it is over hunted for its horn. Write "habitat destruction" in the correct place. The last animal in our chart is the snow leopard. The snow leopard is found in Central Asia. The snow leopard is over hunted for its fur and it is also killed to protect domestic animals. Write "Central Asia" in the correct place. Now let's complete the information for the two plants we have in our chart. The first one, the floating sorrel, is found in South Africa. The main reason it is endangered is habitat destruction. Write "South Africa" in the correct place. The last plant in the chart is the Knowlton cactus. It is found in the Southwestern part of the United States in the states of New Mexico and Colorado. Habitat destruction and over collection have resulted in its being endangered. Write "over collection" in the correct place.

Animal	Habitat	Reasons Endangered
Giant Panda	China	habitat destruction; illegal killing for its fur; illegal capture for zoos
Blue whale	all oceans	over hunted for its blubber, for food, and for whale oil
California condor	Southern California, Arizona	habitat destruction; hunted for sport; poisoned to protect domestic animals
Black rhinoceros	South of Sahara in Africa	habitat destruction; over hunted for its horn
Snow leopard	Central Asia	over hunted for its fur; killed to protect domestic animals

Plant	Habitat	Reasons Endangered
Floating sorrel	South Africa	habitat destruction
Green pitcher plant	Southwestern United States	habitat destruction; overcollection

Task 2.

Listening to Answer Questions Using the Completed Chart

Write short answers, one word or a few words, to answer the following questions you will hear.

1. Which endangered animal is found in all the oceans? (the blue whale)

2. Which two animals are endangered because they are hunted for their fur? (the Giant Panda and the snow leopard)

3. Which two animals are killed to protect domestic animals? (the California condor and the snow leopard)

4. What are the two reasons that the green pitcher plant is endangered? (habitat destruction and over collection)

5. Of the five animals and two plants on the chart, how many are endangered because of habitat destruction? (five)

Listening Factoid #1

According to British ecologist William Sutherland there are more languages in danger of extinction today than there are bird or mammal species in danger of extinction. The results of a study he did recently show that 7.1% of the living languages in the world today are in serious danger of extinction compared to 4.1% of mammal species and 1.9% of bird species. He notes that 58 species of birds today have fewer than 50 living members, but almost six times as many languages have fewer than 50 speakers. He also reports that 306 languages have disappeared since the year 1600, compared with 125 species of birds and 87 species of mammals. [from *Nature* 423, pp. 276–279 (15 May 2003)]

Listening Factoid #2

According to Marilyn vos Savant, who is reported to have the highest IQ of anyone in the world, insects greatly outweigh human beings. Their total weight would be about 29 times the total weight of human beings. She says that for every human being on earth, there are about 200 millions insects! So the next time you see a tiny insect, remember that insects both outweigh us *and* outnumber us. [from *Parade*, June 6, 2004, p. 19]

Credits and Acknowledgments

Page 39   The yoga exercises were based on Activity 1 of *Penguin Functional English*, *Pair Work*, *Student B* by Peter Watcyn-Jones. Penguin Books, 1982.

Page 74   The Kennedy quotes are from David Wallechinsky and Irving Wallace's *The People's Almanac*. New York: Doubleday & Company, 1975.

Page 107   The Endangered Species chart was created based on information in The World Book Encyclopedia. World Book, Inc. a Scott Fetzer Company, Chicago, IL. 2002.

Page 113   Listening Factoid #1 was based on *Reader's Digest Book of Facts*, The Reader's Digest Association, Inc. Pleasantville, New York, 1987, p. 73.

Page 126   The Internet talk was based on Vint Cerf's "How the Internet Really Works" © Vinton G. Cerf, 1995, 1996. Available at http://www.netlingo.com/more/cerfart.html

Page 190   Listening Factoid #1 was based on information from *Nature*, 432 pp. 276–279 (15 May 2003). Listening Factoid #2 was based on information from *Parade*, June 6, 2004, p. 19.

Photo Credits

Chapter 1
Page 2: © Leonard de Selva/CORBIS

Chapter 2
Page 8: ©Roger Ressmeyer/CORBIS

Chapter 3
Page 14: © Doug Pensinger/Getty

Chapter 4
Page 22: © Brand X Pictures/Alamy

Chapter 5
Page 28: © Royalty-Free/CORBIS

Chapter 6
Page 34: © Joseph Sohm; ChromoSohm Inc./CORBIS

Chapter 7
Page 42: © Warren Bolster/Getty

Chapter 8
Page 48: Image Shop/CORBIS;
Page 48 right: © Photodisc Collection/Getty

Chapter 9
Page 54 far left: © Ronnie Kaufman/CORBIS;
Page 54 left: Tim McGuire/CORBIS;
Page 54 right: © SuperStock/Alamy;
Page 54 far right: © Jack Hollingsworth/Getty

Chapter 10
Page 64 left: © Johnny Johnson/Getty;
Page 64 right: © Galen Rowell/CORBIS

Chapter 11
Page 70 left: © CORBIS; **Page 70 right:** © CORBIS
Page 75 top left: © CORBIS; **Page 75 top right:** © Bettmann/CORBIS;
Page 75 bottom left: © CORBIS; **Page 75 bottom right:** © Bettmann/CORBIS

Chapter 12
Page 77 right: © Bettmann/CORBIS; Page 77 left: © Bettmann/CORBIS

Chapter 13
Page 86: © Paul A. Souders/CORBIS

Chapter 14
Page 94: © Lester Lefkowitz/CORBIS

Chapter 15
Page 102 left: © Fritz Polking/Peter Arnold, Inc.;
Page 102 middle: © Kevin Schafer/Peter Arnold, Inc.;
Page 102 right: © BIOS/Peter Arnold, Inc.